MEMOIR OF A VISIONARY:
Antonia Pantoja

Antonia Pantoja

Editor's Note by Henry A. J. Ramos

Arte Público Press
Houston, Texas

This volume is made possible through grants from the Charles Stewart Mott Foundation, the Ewing Marion Kauffman Foundation, the Rockefeller Foundation, and the City of Houston through The Cultural Arts Council of Houston, Harris County.

Recovering the past, creating the future

Arte Público Press
University of Houston
452 Cullen Performance Hall
Houston, Texas 77204-2004

Cover design by Giovanni Mora
Cover art courtesy of Antonio Matorell

Pantoja, Antonia
    Memoir of a Visionary: Antonia Pantoja / Antonia Pantoja.
        p.   cm.
    Includes bibliographical references.
    ISBN 155885-385-5 (alk. paper)
    ISBN 155885-365-0 (hardcover)
    1. Pantoja, Antonia. 2. Puerto Rican women—United States—Biography. 3. Puerto Ricans—United States—Biography. 4. Political activists—United States—Biography. 5. Social workers—United States—Biography. 6. Puerto Rican youth—United States—Social conditions—20th century. 7. Puerto Ricans—United States—Social conditions—20th century. 8. Puerto Ricans—New York (State)—New York—Societies, etc. 9. Social action—New York (State)—New York—History—20th century. 10. Social action—United States—History—20th century. I. Title.
    E184.P85 P36 2002
    305.868'7295073'092—dc21   2001056695
                                                                                              CIP

♾ The paper used in this publication meets the requirements of the American National Standard for Information Sciences—Permanence of Paper for Printed Library Materials, ANSI Z39.48-1984.

2 3 4 5 6 7 8 9 0 1   10 9 8 7 6 5 4 3 2 1

This book is dedicated to my friend and partner, Wilhelmina Perry. She has been by my side through the pains, glory, and excitement of life. This book could not have been completed without her constant encouragement and direct assistance.

Table of Contents

Acknowledgments

The process of writing this book would have been a laborious and unrewarding task without the contributions that I have received from friends and coworkers Antonio Díaz-Royo, Wilhelmina Perry, Lillian Jiménez, and Anne Gardon. They were instrumental in initially assisting me in organizing my thoughts and the book as it evolved. Their guidance and reflections helped me through the frightening and exciting adventure of traveling inward to discover the self while still telling the story of my actions in the world. They along with Sonia Nieto, Mary Francis Berry, and Mary Marshall Clark read the first version of this book. Their reactions and wise criticism helped me realize that my memoirs are an important contribution to a critical look at the Puerto Rican community of New York.

Throughout the writing process, I was assisted by many others who helped me with research, some provided documents from their personal files while others participated in interviews offering memories, analysis, and perspectives of the work we did together. These included the original group members of the Hispanic Young Adult Association (HYAA) and the Puerto Rican Association for Community Affairs (PRACA), the first Madrinas of ASPIRA, the first ASPIRA students and club presidents, founding staff and board members of the Puerto Rican Forum and ASPIRA, and the first staff and selected board members of Universidad Boricua.

Lillian Jiménez is deserving of my gratitude and appreciation for coordinating and producing tapings with her coworkers Linda Silva and Juan Rodríguez.

My warmest thanks to my friend Antonio Díaz-Royo who provided support and encouragement as I revisited, worked through and finally wrote about some difficult periods in my life.

I wish to acknowledge the valuable time and contributions that were offered by my long time coworkers and friends Luis Nuñez, Toni Galvez, Blanca Cedeño, Yolanda Sánchez and Luis Álvarez, who have enough stories to write their own books.

I wish to thank Antonio Matorell who generously offered his art for the cover of this book.

I also offer my appreciation to the Ford and the Rockefeller Foundations who offered support in this endeavor. The monies received from both Foundations was used to hire two research assistants, one in Puerto Rico and another in New York, and a professional video crew to assist with research and documentation activities. All documents and copies of videos that resulted from this project will be donated to the Center for Puerto Rican Studies at Hunter College in the City University of New York.

Lastly, I thank Mr. Antonio Romero and Ms. Janice Petrovich of the Ford Foundation and Dr. Tomás Ybarra Frausto of the Rockefeller Foundation for their assistance to me during this project.

Foreword

It is very odd to start the foreword to a book by saying I was not intending to write it, but this is exactly what I have to say since I never considered writing about myself.

As life would have it, one day in 1998 while I was living in Puerto Rico, a young man who had been a member of ASPIRA (an "aspirante") was visiting with me. We talked about our lives as people who consider themselves New Yorkers. He asked many questions about my arrival in New York City, why I emigrated, what my school life in Puerto Rico was like, why I never married, what I liked and disliked about our culture, my philosophy of life, and many other topics. At the same time, he told me about himself. In this conversation on the beach, we, the young and the aged, exchanged confidences and experiences. I had never revealed myself this way before. Suddenly, he said, "One day you will die and no one will know how important your life has been for other Puerto Ricans in the city and for the city's development." I responded that I had thought about writing a book about ASPIRA, the work that I consider my most significant. He replied that the story of ASPIRA would not be enough. I had to write my entire life story, starting from my very humble origins up to receiving the Presidential Medal of Freedom from President Bill Clinton in 1996. My life, he said, was important because it provided an example for many young Puerto Rican New Yorkers who had very few mentors, heroes, and important figures to emulate.

After this conversation, I requested and received a grant from the Ford Foundation to launch me on my adventure: writing a book. As I write today, I have received a second grant from the Rockefeller Foundation. This project ended my retirement. For the last two years, I have written every day early in the morning. Only appointments with people who are important to this work have interrupted me. This book has given birth to a number of side projects: the beginning of an archival project of letters, documents, and other materials from me and others that we anticipate will eventually become a part of the Center for Puerto Rican Studies of Hunter College in collaboration with Puerto Ricans who wish to establish a Puerto Rican Historical Society in New York. A second project will be a series of audiovisual tapes that preserve the history and recollections of the many people involved in developing institutions serving Puerto Ricans in New York. A third project is the formation of an alumni association of Aspirantes. Each of these "children of the memoirs" has taken off under the direction of people who have contributed greatly to my life's work.

There are puzzling questions that I ask myself, but I do not find satisfying answers: "How was I able to accomplish so much?" I believe that I have accomplished so much because I have guarded my integrity and my connections to my community. I have never accepted gifts and promotions that I felt I had not earned and deserved. If I had not guided my life by these principles of integrity and honesty, I believe that I might have lived a life of self-serving mockery.

I complete this work feeling proud and satisfied with what these memoirs will say about me.

Editor's Note

One of contemporary America's first indications of the emergence of Latinos as a significant segment of U.S. society came with the large-scale migration of Puerto Ricans to many of the nation's northeastern cities, and especially to New York City, following World War II. Seeking employment and educational opportunities, more than a million Puerto Ricans found their way north to the continental United States during the war and subsequent years. With this migration came the need for new community leadership and institutions to bridge cultural, linguistic, and material divides that separated the growing numbers of Puerto Rican migrants (who had been U.S. citizens since 1917) from mainstream U.S. society.

Antonia Pantoja emerged during the 1960s as a leading figure in establishing the Puerto Rican community's place in regional and national policy-making. Pantoja was born in 1921 in Puerta de Tierra, a slum of the Old San Juan City in Puerto Rico, and raised in Barrio Obrero, a worker housing community located on the outskirts of the island's capital city. She was initially introduced to progressive politics through the work of her grandfather, a union leader employed at the American Tobacco Company. But Pantoja's real politicization came after she migrated to New York City to pursue her interest in education and the larger world beyond Puerto Rico.

Working odd jobs and experimenting with New York's bohemian culture of artists and musicians, community organizers, and intellectuals, Pantoja found direction and purpose in activist scholarship and youth organizing. She quickly emerged as a strong leader, helping to pull together the first generation of Puerto Rican youth activists on the U.S. mainland to expand social and educational opportunities for

Puerto Ricans in and around New York City. These activities led her to become a staff member of an important new city commission on intergroup relations. In time, Pantoja's work on the commission helped to produce two of the most critically important national Puerto Rican civil rights groups of the twentieth century: The Puerto Rican Forum (an umbrella organization of major Puerto Rican leaders and groups), and ASPIRA (today, the nation's premier educational advancement organization focused on Puerto Rican community educational rights).

As the founding executive director of ASPIRA, Pantoja quickly established herself as a leading figure in minority America's nascent quest for educational intervention and support models designed to address the growing needs and inequalities facing students of color. Her leadership was instrumental in taking the New York school system to the U.S. Supreme Court, to protect the language and learning rights of Puerto Ricans and other Spanish-speaking students in New York public schools.

Following her leadership of ASPIRA, Pantoja went on to pursue a series of organizational and higher educational positions that enabled her to expand her leadership to the realms of community development and political advocacy, both in the U.S. and Puerto Rico. Through this work, Pantoja and her colleagues helped to advance new notions of community-based and community-responsive social investment. Her work captured the attention of U.S. politicians no less influential than former U.S. senator Robert F. Kennedy and former New York City mayor John Lindsay, as well as various dignitaries throughout the Americas.

In each of her illustrious pursuits over the years, Antonia Pantoja has broken new ground. She has been not only an impressive advocate of minority and migrant rights, but also a feminist (well before it was fashionable to be characterized as such), innovator (building critical new organizations and concepts along her way), and role model for countless progressive scholars and community builders. Recognizing her many contributions to U.S. and Latin American culture, former President Bill Clinton honored Pantoja in 1996 with the prestigious Presidential Medal of Freedom, the highest award an American president can bestow upon a civilian in recognition of exemplary public service.

The memoir that follows offers Pantoja's reflections on her fascinating and important journey from the impoverishment of her childhood to her humble beginnings in New York and to her international acclaim as a community leader and scholar. In this work, Pantoja recounts in her own words the major benchmarks of her journey, which reflect the larger experiences of New York-area Puerto Ricans, the so-called "Nuyoricans," who helped to put the national Latino community on the map for many Americans during the 1960s and 1970s. In her analysis of this journey, Pantoja helps to put into perspective the critical, if still not fully realized, dreams achieved by Puerto Ricans on the mainland during the past five decades. She writes:

> If you consider that the largest wave of Puerto Ricans came to New York starting in 1945, our group has been in the city for only fifty-five years [a relatively brief historical period]. During these fifty-five years . . . we who came without the knowledge of English, few skills, and no economic resources have been able to accomplish many important projects and build many institutions. We have educated a leadership that has been instrumental in helping our group to obtain rights; we have taken a case to the Supreme Court to force the [New York City] Board of Education to teach [our] children in two languages; we have established accredited institutions of higher learning; elected persons to city council, state senators, representatives in Congress . . . Considering that we came to this country with many odds against us, I believe that we have done well in a short period of time, given the realities that we faced . . .

Dr. Antonia Pantoja's contributions to this progress have been many and formidable. We are pleased and honored to include this volume, *Memoir of a Visionary: Antonia Pantoja*, as a leading entry in our Hispanic Civil Rights Series. With major support from funders, including the Charles Stewart Mott Foundation, the Ewing Marion Kauffman Foundation, and the Rockefeller Foundation, the Series will produce more than twenty works over the coming years, chronicling the leaders, the organizations, and the events that have shaped U.S. civil rights and social justice from a Latino perspective. These works will seek especially to educate younger readers, many of whom are being exposed to this history for the first time, as well as more adult general readers interested in the field, about this critical, yet heretofore largely overlooked aspect of American history. The series will add new perspectives on what it means to be an American at a time when increasing diversity and multiculturalism make it essential for all of us to expand our notions of the American experience and community.

Antonia Pantoja's epic story of public service, social justice advocacy, and intellectual innovation will contribute mightily to the public record and establish itself as a staple of curricula, library collections, and community discourse across the United States for years to come.

Henry A. J. Ramos
Executive Editor
Hispanic Civil Rights Series

Introduction

In writing this book, I realized that in great measure one becomes the person one wishes to make oneself. However, there are some given factors and realities that must be taken into consideration, but one must not allow these to become limiting obstacles. Some of these limitations can be seen as insurmountable obstacles, but when viewed as part of one's constantly changing reality, they can become enhancing and transporting experiences. For example, I was born on an island. The sea was a constant presence in my life. The island with its beaches and coastlines could have limited me, but instead I saw it in terms of the world that lay beyond. The sea was a promise out there. Contemplating the sea and its horizon, its vastness, its overwhelming size provoking fear and respect, provided my first adolescent questioning and my search for the meaning of life. I spent long hours pondering in front of the sea, asking such questions as: "Why am I alive?" "Why must I die?" I would respond to myself: "I want to be me forever. I do not want to be part of a fish or the chemicals that will make a tree." The answers provided by science did not satisfy me. Neither did the religious explanations that offered eternal life and resurrection on some future judgment day.

Coming into contact with writers who were inspired by the sea offered me a perspective. I delighted in Julia de Burgos's "Man River," in her poem "El Río Grande de Loiza," (Loiza's Great River), which spills over into the sea and is able to kiss and caress other people on the other shores of the world.

Through literature, I later found a poet who rejoiced and philosophized contemplating the sea. Pedro Salinas, the Spanish poet, wrote his beautiful poem "El Contemplado" (The Beholden) about our sea, and requested to be buried in San Juan's cemetery where he could behold that sea forever.

When I come into San Juan through the most beautiful road that I have ever traveled, Ponce de León Avenue, bordered on its right by that sea until it disappears, hidden by the old colonial wall, I become the mesmerized beholder of Salinas's poem. My reverie and enchantment is broken by the memory brought to mind by black children from the nearby slum, playing in the water. These are the children, descendants of sad Yoruba princesses and furious Cafre fishermen, who never had the knowledge of why they were kidnapped and enslaved on the other side of that sea. These children will never know that their present lives are a reflection of that captivity—an enslavement that resulted in their present subordination.

Reading philosophy later on in my life, I began to formulate a philosophy of life that offered me a guiding core of beliefs to live by. The readings of Kierkegaard, Ortega y Gasset, Hostos, Freire, Fannon, Menninger, Fromm, but above all Miguel de Unamuno, influenced the building of my philosophy of life. As time has gone by and experiences have seasoned my understanding of the ideas of these philosophers and psychiatrists, I have been able to develop a core of guiding principles for my work and life experiences.

Many of my beliefs are influenced by the realization that there are two very important events in one's life: the fact that we are born and the inescapable reality that we will die. Then, the important question becomes: What do you do with the space and time created between these two events? A second important realization at the core of my beliefs is the complicated yet simple knowledge that the nature of reality, of facts, of truth, is not one, but many. Realities vary and change their shape and appearance for each of us. The third important discovery that is a foundation and at the core of my thinking is the inevitable fact that I do not live alone, but that I am interdependent with others. I was nurtured to be who I am, and I am responsible and accountable. I affect and am affected by a community of others. Fourth, and the last idea I will state (although I do not mean that I have exhausted all the sources of my beliefs), is the discovery that change is ever-present in life. However, this fact makes life an exciting adventure because there is no closure in the ever-evolving self, and the beginning is the end and the end is the beginning. . . .

   Because of these beliefs and personal values, I want to live a life of commitment to the human community for the betterment of all human beings. I want to live a passionate life (as contrasted to a luke-warm existence) dedicated to study and evolving knowledge and a life of actions based on that knowledge—a life of praxis. I want to live a life in pursuit of justice, beauty, creativity that potentially emerges at each step as I emerge, change, begin, end, and begin again with oth-ers. I will participate in the making and remaking, in the naming and renaming of our world. I will also participate in changing those situa-tions of injustice and inequality that I will encounter. These beliefs permeate my relation to others and my work in the community. They are not empty, hollow phrases. My life has been one of action, learn-ing, and teaching, a life of building with others, a life of fighting injus-tice and trying to change conditions and relations that are wrong because they deny people their rights and destroy their potentialities. I consider myself an educator, a teacher. However, by teacher, I mean one who engages with the learner and becomes a teacher/learner.

First Part

Toward a Clear Identity
(1922-1944)

It was September 9, 1996, and I was flying from San Juan, Puerto Rico, to Washington, D.C., to be one of the recipients of the Presidential Medal of Freedom from William Jefferson Clinton, president of the United States. As I sat in the airplane thinking about this event in which I was about to participate, many pieces of my life pushed through in my mind. One of these thoughts repeated itself. *I am seventy-five years old! How does this recognition come to me at this age? Am I really deserving of it? Who am I to receive such recognition from the United States? Who am I?*

I am the same person whom my aunt taught to read in the living room of our old house in Barrio Obrero before I was five years old. I am the same person who used to walk miles to high school with holes in the soles of her shoes. I am the same person who was pulled out of her first year of high school because the doctors, who tested all students in the school, found tuberculosis in her lungs. I am the same person who would go on horseback to teach in a rural school in the mountains of our island.

As I sat in the plane on my trip to Washington, D.C., enumerating my work with my community in the resolution of problems suffered by us and by others who are excluded, I concluded that I did deserve the medal and that I should feel the satisfaction of being recognized for my work while I was still alive.

The next morning in an impressive room at the White House, President Bill Clinton placed a medal over my head, and, in doing so, he praised my work with my community, with special recognition for

1

my work with ASPIRA.

When I was a small child attending school in the second grade, every time I had to talk or answer questions about my parents' name, I was caught in a state of fear because I did not know if I would make a mistake. I had to first stop and think, "Who is my mother?" Was she the old lady that I called Mamá who was actually my grandmother? Or was it Alejandrina, my mother by birth? This turmoil and nervousness would be in me before I could answer the question. I would always end up asking myself, "Who is my mother? Who is my father?" The nervousness and embarrassment would lead to my silence, because I did not know my father's name.

Other children answered immediately. I worried that I would appear stupid to my teachers. I was always concerned about being seen as stupid because I wanted to be viewed as an intelligent person. Soon the moment came when I decided not to be caught in the confusion any longer. I was eight years old. I announced to my family that I would take the birth date of September 13, 1921. With this act, I became clearly and without a doubt Antonia Pantoja Acosta, daughter of Conrado Pantoja Santos and Luisa Acosta Rivera. However, I requested that my family celebrate my birth date at home on June 13. Since my actual birthdate was 1922, I was making myself one year older, but I liked that. I told myself to always remember that my mother was Alejandrina Pantoja.

This struggle for identity began and continued for years into my adult life. How did all this confusion begin? I was born the child of Alejandrina, an unwed mother. Out of shame, my grandparents took the responsibility of bringing me into their life as their daughter by registering me in the official documents on a different date than the actual birth date. As I understand the story, my grandfather had a friend who worked in the registry, and with his assistance, I was registered again a year earlier. I do not know why the birth date was changed. I can only guess that an entirely fictitious date was chosen to disassociate me from the illegitimate birth date.

The confusion about me would continue as others spoke about me in my presence. They would stumble over how old I was or how my first name, Antonia, was chosen. To give a name to a child in a Catholic country, you needed to consult the official church book of saints to locate the saint of your birthday. June 13 is St. Anthony's day, so I was named Antonia. No one ever explained my situation to me. I carried the different stories inside me and tried over many years, from time to time, to find an appropriate moment to ask my mother who my father was and why she had such difficulty dealing with the reality of me in her life. I never did. To this day, I regret not having had this conversation with her. I still feel angry at myself for having resorted to the indirectness and mendacity that is so prevalent in the Puerto Rican culture that prevents the asking of questions considered embarrassing to others.

These strange circumstances around my parentage did not, however, totally destroy my sense of worth and dignity. My grandmother would constantly tell people the story of how I was born. I was present several times when she told people that I was born in a *zurrón* (a bag made of skin). I tried to find out the meaning of being born in a *zurrón*. Someone whom I do not remember told me that children were born in a sack full of a liquid when they came out of their mother's body. It turns out that being born in a *zurrón* meant that you came out of your mother's body in the sack that did not break to release the liquid. The midwife had to be fast to break the sack so that the baby would not suffocate during the delivery. I learned that I was in jeopardy at birth and that the midwife had saved my life. From then on, my grandmother would always end the story by saying that I was a person with a special destiny. I did not know what this meant, but I imagined that it meant that my experiences would be different from those of other people. When my grandmother tried to place a pendant around my neck with the dried *zurrón* in an embroidered bag, I refused vehemently to submit to her efforts. They said that the bag represented my luck because I was spared death. My grandmother put the bag away with her things, and I never knew what became of it.

My grandmother, who had a great influence on me during those early years, truly believed that I had a special destiny. She would call me into the parlor when visitors came and she would say, "Toñita, show them your hands. You see, she has a special destiny. You can see it in her hands." Who could not believe this type of *vaticinio* (prophecy)? I believed my grandmother, and I acted the part.

When I remembered this, years later, I realize that my grandmother recognized early on that I was a child with great curiosity, intelligence, and sensitivity. She could not voice this in these words and could only translate it into "a special destiny." From very early in my childhood, I would speak about events and relationships that I would observe. I never used baby talk. I was the kind of child who would comment on events and participate in conversations adults were conducting.

My friend Mina tells me that I am an excellent storyteller with an amazing ability to remember in detail incidents of my early life. This is true. I am amazed by this myself. As I reflect on the extent of my recall, I attribute it to the fact that I lived my very early years as an observer of my surroundings. I lived as a child with the ability to observe, analyze, and interpret what was happening to me and others in my family. My life as a young child was full of much activity, tangled relationships, and the unresolved questions surrounding my birth. As a child, I needed to make decisions and find solutions to issues and events that were never addressed by the adults in my world. I knew that I must be the maker of who I would become. The stories of the members of my family and my reactions and interactions with them have impressed upon me, both directly and indirectly, the values, attitudes, and ideas that have shaped my entire life. In spite of the paucity in their own lives, they transmitted to me a sense of value for myself and a determination to be self-sufficient and independent. These persons helped to develop and nurture the adult I would become.

Grandfather

At this point in my life, as I remember my grandmother and grandfather, I realize how very important they were in my becoming who I am. These two people made their daughter's illegitimate child one of their children. My grandfather, who is more an invented figure in my memory, was to me a generous and loving man. He was also an intelligent human being who made himself by learning, reading, and discussing with his friends issues that were important to his life. He was a foreman in his factory. Grandfather talked about the *sindicatos* (labor unions). He owned many pamphlets and booklets. I remember some that were training books from unions in Spain and France and a booklet of Lenin's, "Letters to the Workers." My early awareness of the rights of workers began with my grandfather's reading material. One incident of his union life was deeply important in my mind. It was about seven-thirty at night. Several men brought my grandfather into the house. His feet were wrapped in large gauze with a yellow medicine showing through. They said that strikebreakers had come to the *friquitín* (a place where fritters, made of flour and codfish or made of green plantains with meat, were cooked in very hot oil) and had thrown a large iron cauldron full of hot lard at my grandfather. Friends had taken him to the community health clinic to receive medical attention for the burns on his feet. The doctor said that, miraculously, his abdomen and legs were not seriously burned because he was wearing heavy denim coveralls. His feet, however, were severely burned from the hot lard that went into his shoes. Everyone reported that the strike was on! Strikebreakers and guards from the company had beaten many men. Finally, after many weeks, the news came from the workers on the picket line that large trucks had come to the factory buildings and men had moved the machinery and furnishings in crate boxes. These boxes were to be removed from the island on a freighter ship. Congregating in the street in front of my house with a large group of defeated workers, I heard my grandfather say, "The sons of bitches, bastards. All we were asking for was a few cents more to feed our families." I will never forget the company's name: The American Tobacco Company. The workers had won their strike, but the company removed the source of employment from Puerto Rico. From then on, years of hunger and very bad economic and health conditions came upon our family because my grandfather, my Aunt Juanita, and my mother were unemployed. This was not only the beginning of the destruction of one family, but the situation befell many families in Barrio Obrero.

I remember my grandfather as a dapper dresser. He wore spats over his shoes, a vest, and a beautiful watch that had a chain you could see across his vest. Whenever he went out, he would use a cane that had a head of a dog with two little red stones for eyes. He was a small man. His hair was thin and fine. As a child, I thought that he was a handsome man who was very proud. He had lots of friends who liked him very much.

My grandfather lived until I was six years old. His death created a big difference in our lives. When Grandfather worked, I can remember that we had electricity in the house. He would go shopping, and a young delivery boy would bring a box full of food back to our family. Grandfather showed affection toward Grandmother, although she would shy away from his overtures. When he came home from work and she served dinner, he complained very loudly, half in jest and half angry, that he did not get enough food because she was always giving food to our neighbors on both sides of the house. He would say, "I am a hardworking man. I need a large pork chop or a steak. This little thing will fit in my molar." While he did this, my grandmother would hum a tune and walk back and forth from the kitchen to the dining area. I often observed these interactions and the connections between them, and I concluded that this is a very effective way to deal with men when they become angry: ignore them and go about your business. Thus, at an early age, I became aware of power dynamics in male and female relationships and of the need for women to learn how to deal effectively with men in power situations.

Every evening after eating his dinner, Grandfather would move to a rocking chair in the living room to read the newspaper, smoke a cigar, and drink his cup of black coffee. I would sit nearby to wait until he would call me to give me his cup in which he would leave a little coffee with a lot of sugar from the many spoonfuls that he would use. While I waited for him to finish, the large smoke rings rising over the newspaper fascinated me. I also watched very intensely as large gray ash formed at the end of his cigar and anticipated its fall to the floor. These were very peaceful and happy moments for me. One day he said to me, "I want you to remember that you carry my name. I want you to honor it!" This is a memory that I will never forget. Grandfather always called me Toñita, a diminutive name for Antonia, but when he was angry he called me Antonia with a thundering voice. I respected and loved him very much.

Grandfather was the strong pillar that held the family together. He and his children—Conradito, José Belén (who died from pneumonia after going to New York with my mother), Aunt Juanita, and my mother—all worked at the American Tobacco Company in Puerta de Tierra. The whole family worked there except for Aunt Magui, who usually worked at home, but once worked at a hair-net factory.

Grandfather's income as a skilled worker was the basic income to support the household. Although my uncle continued to support the family after my grandfather's death, he seemed to earn less money. When Grandfather died, our house deteriorated. There was never enough food. Meat disappeared from our meals. Rarely was there any milk. In addition to these changes in the family's meals, the furniture in the house began to disappear. I could never determine if it was sold or it just fell into disrepair and was discarded. We had few types of linen for the beds. I had a pillow and a sheet that was washed again and again. During the time that my grandfather lived, we were not rich, but I had a sense that I was being taken care of very well. With his death, a new period began. While Grandfather's death brought many changes inside the home, we remained the Pantoja family, and the respect that he had earned continued to be given to us.

Grandmother

My grandmother was the person with whom I spent much time. She died after I became an adult, so I have memories of her from my childhood and into my adult life. She was cantankerous and critical of everybody. She was not loving. You could feel a distance from her. As a child, I would challenge her, and I knew that she took things from me that she would not take from anyone else. I would contradict her and question her criticism of me.

My grandmother was a frail, skinny, small woman, darker than her mother. She objected very strongly to anyone taking a picture of her. She was very superstitious. I think that she carried ideas from the old days when she was a young woman. Sometimes, she would take me to her sister, Damiana, who lived by Bus Stop 25 on a street that they called "La Revuelta del Diablo" (The Devil's Revolt). Damiana owned a farm with a large wooden house and many children lived with her. Much later, I would learn how my family had no legal papers of ownership, and lost this land only to become renters and eventually to be displaced. The story of their loss of land is very similar to the loss of land by African Americans in the South and Mexican Americans in the Southwest. The area is now heavily developed with beautiful homes and a large government center.

I liked my grandmother even though I was critical of her ideas about religion, and I thought that she was wrong in her treatment of my aunt Magui. Nonetheless, she spoiled me and let me know that she preferred me over her other grandchildren. She took me with her to places I was not supposed to go. Although she would say that she was a Catholic if you asked her about her religion, she did not go to church. She attended spiritualist meetings, and I accompanied her. We would leave in the early evening, and she would instruct me to bring my school bench. When I heard this, I knew we were going to a seance at the house of Juan Ojai. Juan Ojai was a very tall, very black, very handsome man who was known for his curative faculties and for presiding over seances. He held the seances in a large living room with a long table in the middle that had six chairs on each side and two chairs on each end. The table was covered by a white tablecloth with a glass of water and a vase of white flowers in the middle and two candles on each side of the vase. Juan Ojai would sit at one end of the table with his back to the entrance door. On his side sat one "medium." (A medium is a person, usually a woman, who has the special faculties of being able to offer herself as an instrument through which the dead could speak with the living.) A second medium sat at the opposite end of the table. The entrance to the room was covered with a curtain that was drawn once the seance began. The flowers were removed, the candles lit, and the electric light was turned off. The room would be full of men and women, young and old. I would be the only child present, sitting on the bench behind my grandmother. When the lights were turned off, Juan Ojai would begin by calling all good spirits to come in. At the same time, he would tap the glass of water with a pencil. The rhythmic taps on the glass and calls to the spirits to come and speak with their loved ones were interrupted by cries and sighs from the two mediums. The mediums' sighs and cries meant that a spirit was trying to communicate through them. The first few times that I attended these sessions, I was petrified with fear waiting for the spirits to speak through the women. Juan Ojai would coax one of the spirits to come in, and the woman next to him would begin talking in a low, hoarse voice like a man. During the seances, various spirits came to bring messages to persons who were present. They were brothers, husbands, sons, and daughters of the participants who had died but needed to speak with the family before going to their resting place. After speaking, the spirits would stop lingering in the house where they had lived or stop hovering around the living relative. Some spirits spoke softly and behaved well. Others made the mediums fall from their chairs, hit people, or threaten to hit them. The bad spirits had to be scolded by Juan Ojai. The people sitting adjacent to the mediums would have to hold them down. Juan Ojai would threaten to punish the bad spirits, but I never saw him do this. Grandmother could not tell me how he did it.

After accompanying Grandmother several times on these adventures, I began to be disruptive by giggling when the spirits made the mediums sigh and cry. Juan Ojai became very angry and said that someone was interfering "with the connection." At one time, I laughed so loud that he stopped the session and turned on the light. My grandmother had to leave and swore she would not bring me with her again. This incident broke a certain special connection that she had had with me. For me, the seances developed an attitude of openness and curiosity about the possibility of the spirits of the dead being able to affect the lives of the living.

Certain ways about my grandmother always personified for me aspects of Puerto Rican culture of which I was critical. I felt that my grandmother was unjust and abused her power to force her children to do things without regard for their feelings of well-being. She did not allow Magui to marry Johnny, her boyfriend, because his fingernails were always full of black dirt from fixing cars. She was critical of him because he did not finish school and had dropped out before graduating from elementary school. The real reason, I thought, that Grandmother opposed the marriage was because she wanted Magui to stay at home and work to bring income into the house. This type of exploitation was common, especially of the youngest female child.

There were other reasons for my mistrusting her. I knew very early in my life that my mother had a very bad relationship with her family. Her pregnancy and my birth had created a problem with both her parents to the point that she had moved away from the family home and abandoned me. Growing up, I called my grandmother "Mamá," but there was no warmth or open demonstrations of love coming from her that I could count on. She was a rather elusive person who was not really interested in caring for one more child after she had finished rearing her own children. This meant a double rejection for me—one from my mother and another from my grandmother. I grew up a lonely child, spending time with my toys and my dog. I would often sit under the table with my dog and talk with him.

Grandmother was a good storyteller. A story that she told repeatedly was about the bombardment of San Juan by the American warships when Puerto Rico was invaded by the United States in the late 1800s. Her family lived on Calle Cruz in the old walled city of San Juan. Grandmother told us over and over again, "when we heard the cannon shots, I grabbed my baby and ran with the other neighbors away from the city to what was then called *el monte* (the wilderness)." This area is now called Santurce. It was impossible to get any more details from her about this since she refused to say any more. I developed a strong resentment against the American navy that had bombarded us and made our people run for safety. This story of the Americans would have a follow-up when I was in elementary school. I remember the marches in the plaza where young people from the neighborhood would march like soldiers, in white pants and black shirts, holding wooden sticks in the manner that one would hold a rifle. They would be drilled in a military fashion as they marched all around the plaza. Everyone spoke about the fact that these were soldiers of the Nationalist Party, the military organization of Don Pedro Albizu Campos, who planned to obtain the independence of Puerto Rico from the United States.

At one point, there was a demonstration of the high school students coming into our elementary school to pick us up to march to San Juan. Albizu's political party organized this demonstration. The evening before, someone had come to the school and put a flag of

Puerto Rico on the school flagpole, applying grease to the pole so that no one could climb the pole and take the flag down. It was prohibited by law to fly the flag of Puerto Rico.

We were very excited, and when the high school students came to our school the next morning, my whole class left to join the marchers. As I walked out of the gates of the school and joined the long line of marching students, I felt a hand pull me out of the demonstration. It was my uncle, who had come to see if I was marching. He pulled me out and said, "Do you want to be killed? You cannot do this." When I got home, they told me that I was too small to be engaged in such activities. The next few weeks after this march, there was an investigation in which we were interviewed as a group, and afterwards, the principal and his assistant interviewed us individually to find out who had joined the march. No one spoke or gave the names of others.

Those were days of political turmoil in Puerto Rico, which came to a head with the Ponce Massacre in 1937, in which the local police opened fire against marchers in the city of Ponce. I knew about this because it was all over the newspapers. That evening, I heard some noise in my house. A group of men had brought a wounded man through our back door and placed him in a back bedroom. The next morning, I learned that it was Urbano, the son of family friends, who had been in the Ponce march and had wounds on his legs and back. The next day, he was removed by the back door and taken to a doctor. He was one of the young people who had marched in the plaza. Shortly after this incident, Urbano disappeared and I never saw him again. This was a secret that was never discussed in my home or in the neighborhood. We had hidden Urbano from the police. Nothing like this ever happened again.

Later, I learned that my stepfather was an active member of the Socialist Party in Loíza. This was known by everyone. During one election, the Socialist Party joined with the Liberal and Republican Parties in something that the three parties called Tripartitas.

Only afterwards, when I was living in the United States, did I understand the full significance of my experiences with early political events and persons.

As I have stated, in the years of 1934 and 1935, it was a crime to fly the Puerto Rican flag. People were afraid to talk about the United States having invaded Puerto Rico in 1898 or to discuss the Ponce Massacre. One could come under surveillance for expressions of patriotism for Puerto Rico.

On Sunday mornings, my grandmother combed my hair, dressed me, and sent me to church. Before leaving, she would place my veil and money in my hands. The money was to be given as an offering when the basket was passed. I would go next door to call on Paquita, my friend and companion in many adventures. We would leave for church and walk down the main avenue toward the church. Every Sunday the same small drama would be played out. I would say to Paquita, "Let us walk to San Juan and not go to church." She would answer, "San Juan is so far and I'll get tired." I would then promise that we would catch the bus when she got tired, because we both had the money given to us for church. After a weak opposition, Paquita would agree, and we would pass by the church and continue on our walk to San Juan, which was indeed far from our home in Barrio Obrero. We would walk down Avenida Ponce de León. In those days, this avenue had many large and beautiful homes. On the way, we taunted dogs to make them bark. We stopped at houses with gardens and picked roses to eat their petals as we walked. We sat in doorways and at bus stops to rest. Hot and perspiring, we usually reached San Juan about three hours later. We sat on benches at Plaza Colón, the first plaza when you reach the city. After making several attempts to get lost, but not succeeding because the old city is so small that you can always see the bay or the ocean from every street, I would suggest that we go to eat ice cream at "La Bombonera." A café with a soda fountain, famous for its homemade ice cream and its homemade french-fried potatoes, and that is what we always ate. The bowl of fried potatoes would be placed on the counter for customers to eat free of charge. When we finished, I would suggest, as I did every Sunday, that we not pay, since we were so small that the counter would hide us when we got off the stools, and we could leave the store without being noticed. Paquita would enjoy herself so much that she would put up no resistance, and we would leave without paying. I never really could tell if the owners knew that we did this every Sunday. After leaving the store, we were so tired that we would go directly to the bus and return home. This adventure was never discovered until several months later when the bishop came to confirm those children who were "ready." "Ready" meant that you could answer questions that he posed, because you had learned them in catechism classes. A woman who was our neighbor was present and knew that we could not answer the questions correctly. She went to my grandmother's house and told her that we had never been to church on Sundays and had not attended the catechism classes. When I was faced with this, I said to her, "Grandmother, you do not go to church. Why do you want me to go?" She said loudly that I was ill-bred and that she was going to speak with my mother about my behavior. I thought, *You have raised me, so why go to my mother now, if I don't behave?*

Aunt Magui

For much of my growing up years, the household consisted of my grandmother and my aunt. My major conversations were with my Aunt Magui and, later when I went out to play, with other children. With my aunt, I could talk about my mother, my fears and fantasies. She would pick me up and hug me. I would hug her in return with great enthusiasm. I received a sense of the world from her. She would take me on walks with her boyfriend. They would buy me roasted peanuts. To this day, I love peanuts.

Magui was much younger than my mother. She was only sixteen when I was a small child. One of her presents to me was a small dog that she named Otelo because she told me that this was the name of a black prince from Italy. My aunt would buy me the latest little books of fairy tales, which sold for one or two pennies. The children of my neighborhood exchanged these books once we had read them. These were the stories about fairy godmothers, bad witches, and children lost in the forest. I tried to imagine what a forest looked like. At night when I was put to bed, there were spots of lights that entered the house from the streetlights through some holes in the walls. Before falling asleep, I would always wonder if these lights could be the fairy god-mothers or the witches of the stories. Sometimes a firefly would enter the room, and I would follow it around with my eyes. I would invent stories in my mind about fairies and witches that I would later tell Aunt Magui. She would tell me that some spots were fireflies and point out the holes in the house that created lights to dispel my ideas that they were fairies or witches. I often thought that I could catch many fireflies and light up a whole room with their glow.

Aunt Magui occupied a special place in my life. Her given name was María Luisa, but she was called Magui as a nickname of endear-ment. Magui occupied the position of mother in my life. No matter how destructive the experience of being left by my biological mother and the fear and hurt that would be inflicted by Aunt Juanita with her stories about my origins, Aunt Magui's love and care for me gave me a strong sense of well-being.

She was there to console me, to entertain me, dress me, teach me, and answer my many questions. When I was five years old, Aunt Magui organized a school in the living room of our house. Parents would pay a quarter a week for their children to attend. Everybody received a glass of refreshment made of sesame or almond syrup with water and ice. These drinks were called *orchata de almendra o de ajonjolí*. I loved these cold and wonderfully exotic drinks. Every child would bring a small bench from home. I remember that I loved Fer-nando, the young man adopted by my grandmother, who had made me a bench. Under my aunt's teaching, I learned to read and write in Eng-lish and to say some words in French. She taught us songs that I shall never forget: *pollito*—chicken, *gallina*—hen, *lápiz*—pencil, and *pluma*—pen. She taught us *villancicos* or folk songs from Spain, such as *Mambrú se fue a la guerra, qué dolor, qué dolor, qué pena, Mam-brú se fue a la guerra y no sé si volverá*. In French, she taught us "*Alouette, gentile alouette, jete plumerai la tête, et la tête, et la tête, et la tête, alouette, alouette*." I do not know how or when Aunt Magui learned these songs. She was a very intelligent and giving person, and she always consoled me for my mother's long absences.

When my grandmother refused to allow Magui to marry Johnny, her auto mechanic boyfriend, I was very unhappy. Aunt Magui ran away with Johnny anyway, and they went to live in a rooming house near our home. One day, while Johnny was at work, Grandmother went to the room and brought Magui back home. She cried and cried inconsolably. From that day, she refused to eat. She refused to come out of her room and did not speak to anyone. Everyone in the house was upset. Grandmother brought in Juan Ojai, who was also known as a *curandero,* a healer. Juan treated Aunt Magui with what people called *pases,* which are really rubs. He would talk to her and pray, asking her to join him while he rubbed her with leaves of different medicinal plants. He continued these practices for about a week. Then one day, Magui came out of her room, started to speak and eat. This ended a sad episode in the life of Aunt Magui.

Although I was angry at my grandmother's oppression of Aunt Magui, I also began to think about how hard life was for our family and about the contribution that each person made to the well-being of the entire household. Grandmother and Aunt Magui would wash and iron bundles of dirty clothes that they would pick up from families that lived on the other side of the plaza. We all thought that these families were rich because they sent their clothing to be washed and ironed outside of their homes. Magui and Grandmother would pick up the large bundles wrapped in a sheet. These dirty clothes were boiled first in large metal cans in the backyard. The water was mixed with the ashes from the *fogón,* the cement box in the yard where we cooked (since there was no stove in the kitchen). We gathered ashes from burned charcoal that became the bleach for the clothes we washed. The clothes were soaked and boiled over a fire, then pulled out of the hot water and placed on large sheets of tin to get them further bleached by the sun and to get them ready for the rest of the washing process. Each piece of clothing would be soaped with large yellow bars of Octagon soap. The women would scrub each piece on a wooden washboard until all the dirt was gone. Then, the clothes were rinsed, wrung out by hand, and hung in the sun on clotheslines that stretched across the yard. The two women, one old and one young, worked very hard, perspiring profusely from the hot water and fire under the burning sun. Now, as an adult, I can remember thinking how hard the women in my family worked. My view of women has been shaped by images of women engaged in this type of heroic work. The laundering operation would take place on Mondays and Tuesdays. On Wednesdays and Thursdays, they would iron. While my grandmother ironed, she would place me on the bed in front of her. On the bed, I would do all kinds of pirouettes and tricks with my fingers and legs, saying that I was entertaining her. Jumping on the bed, I would say, "Watch me, Mamá, see how I can touch the ceiling," or, "Mamá, see how tall I am?" I would spend hours trying to touch my forehead with my toes and trying to fold into two. She would humor me by saying, "My, how big you are!" or "How talented you are!" Usually, I would fall asleep after long periods of these games while the women continued their work.

Much later when I was an adult living in the United States, I returned to Puerto Rico to visit Aunt Magui in the hospital. She suffered from tuberculosis and diabetes. She had four children, and I would stay with her daughter, Ketty. I helped Ketty and her husband buy a house in one of the new developments so that a room would be set up for Aunt Magui when she left the hospital. She never learned what I had accomplished in New York. She was in and out of the sanatorium. I returned to Puerto Rico on one occasion when she was very ill. This was a very sad time for me. I was with her when she died. She was only in her fifties. I was by her bedside and held her hand. She knew that I was with her. I felt that I had lost a very important piece of myself. But in some way I transferred my love to Ketty's beautiful little boy, Raymundo, who remains an important part of my life.

Other Family Members

My second aunt was Aunt Juanita. I considered her *antipática* (disagreeable, unpleasant). When she came to the house, she would tease me by saying that I did not belong in the family. She would say, "We found you in a garbage can where a *madama* put you. We picked you up and brought you into the house." *Madama* was a derogatory name for an English-speaking black woman from the islands. She would say, "If you look at yourself, you do not look like anyone here." I can remember looking at Aunt Magui and Grandmother to see if I looked like them. I was scared by the fact that I did not seem to look like them. They were all dark. I was light. I would wonder why. I would think, "Maybe I do not belong here. I am different." Aunt Magui would say, "Do not pay attention to Juanita. You are the daughter of our sister, Alejandrina, and you belong here."

Another member of the family was Uncle Conradito. He was uncommunicative, but I still liked him. He was the oldest child after my mother. Sometimes he would take me for walks. When he shaved, I would stand by him and plague him with questions: "Why do you shave? You do not have any hair on your face. I know that you are shaving because you are going out to visit your girlfriend. Are you going to see María?" To all these questions, I would get a grunt or two. I remember that Uncle Conradito taught me how to tie my shoelaces. Although I remember these few kind things, he was like a shadow in the house, not relating much to anyone.

The making of my identity was forged by a combination of all these people and the multiple experiences with them and others. Although I was a child living in very poor circumstances, I also was surrounded by many loving relationships and meaningful experiences that contributed to my being the kind of person that I became. My godfather was one of the persons who brought wonderful experiences to my childhood. My godfather, Martín Ortiz-Padilla, was a linotypist for a newspaper. This made it possible for him to earn a good income and enjoy cultural activities that my family never knew existed. He would visit the house on Saturdays or Sundays. He would bring records of *zarzuelas* (Spanish operettas) or famous operatic selections sung by Enrico Caruso. We still had a Victrola in the house, so he would play the records and talk with me about the music and the famous tenor. No one in my home had ever heard about Enrico Caruso nor did they know anything about opera. I would listen to my godfather's explanations and concentrate on the singing.

Other experiences that my godfather brought to my life were our visits to the theater. He would purchase tickets to the Teatro Tapia when famous theater companies would come from Madrid. I remember seeing "La Malquerida," a famous play that came to the theater. This play had to be read and studied in high school, but I had seen it in live theater. My godfather would also take me for walks along the beach in Cataño, a town across the bay from the old city of San Juan. I would wait with great expectations for these Sunday outings. We would take the bus to San Juan, walk to the piers where the Lancha de Cataño (the Cataño ferry) docked to be boarded for crossing the bay. Godfather would point out the old walls of the city, telling me that they were built by the Spaniards to defend the city from many attacks by English and Dutch war vessels trying to capture the island of Puerto Rico. He would tell me stories of how Chinese workers were brought by Spain to build the walls because they had the experience and skill in building stone walls in China. He would also point to the city's famous buildings, which we could see clearly from the bay, such as the Fortaleza, the governor's mansion. When we finally arrived at the pier in Cataño, we would walk toward the beach. I would pick up seashells of many colors, shapes, and sizes. My collection was very beautiful and varied. Throughout these wonderful days together, I spoke with Martín as if I were an adult, because that was the way he treated me.

My Mother and the Unknown Father

My mother never lived in our household when I was growing up. For me, she was the beautiful, slender, black, mysterious woman. I admired her, and at the same time I resented her absence from my life. In retrospect and in writing this book, I have had to analyze many things about my childhood, especially my feelings about my mother. The admiration that I have always had for my mother is connected to the special place that she held in my grandfather's life. My grandfather loved her and came to her defense whenever my grandmother was critical of her irresponsibility toward me and toward the family. Whenever this would happen, I would feel strongly attached to his opinion in defense of my mother. The resentment of her abandoning me would become intermingled with the emotions that my grandfather and I shared toward my mother. I would struggle with this inconsistency all my life. I can remember that she would stand next to me in front of my grandmother's house on Calle 14, and I would stand next to her on the top of the stairs. As I would lean against her chest, I would feel so fortunate that she was my mother. One day, while this was happening, I said to her, "When I grow up, I am going to earn a lot of money, and I am going to buy you the house that you want. I will live with you in that house." I cannot remember her response. Purchasing a house for my mother was always an ambition. I was able to fulfill this ambition much later in life, when my sister Lydia and I bought her a house in Puerto Rico. She lived in this house after she returned from New York in the 1960s, until her death.

Since my childhood, I was never able to hold onto my mother long enough. I remember asking constantly, "When is she coming?" "Why didn't she come?" "Where does she live?" I felt that she did not want to be with me and that her promises to visit did not matter to her. She would say that she was coming, but often would not show up. Every time that this happened, it was a confirmation that she did not care about me. At these times, I felt that it was good that her mother did not like her. Grandmother always felt angry with my mother because of my birth. At one point when I was still a small child, I remember my grandmother sending me to spend a full day with my mother. I remember the events of the day. While I was visiting my mother, her neighbor's son destroyed a toy that I liked very much. Annoyed by his laughter of glee and his teasing of me, I jumped over the porch fence that divided the two apartments, and I grabbed him and pushed him down the stairs. When his mother came out screaming, my mother also came out to see what had happened. After they argued, my mother grabbed me and brought me into the house and spanked me thoroughly. I cried and cried all afternoon, hoping that my grandmother would come for me early. She did come early and found me sitting in a corner. As soon as she came, I started to cry again, showing her the red marks on my legs where my mother had spanked me. Grandmother was furious, and said that she herself did not spank me, neither could my mother. My grandmother also said that she would not allow me to visit again. They said many angry things to one another, and I heard my mother saying that I was her child and she had the right to spank me when I misbehaved. My grandmother replied that she had cared for me as a baby, and that my real mother had no right to claim herself as mother. My grandmother took me away. I think that I was about eight years old when this incident occurred. I never visited my mother's house again during my childhood years.

As an adult, I came to understand why my mother both loved and resented me. I had been the cause of so much pain in her life that she needed to make herself forgive me for having caused this pain. It was very evident when we were both adults that she had a desire to keep me away from her other children. It took a lifetime for me to be able to understand the entire relationship and her demands that I demonstrate my love for her.

I never knew who my father was. As best as I can understand, I am the child of one of two men, Simón Cruz or Olivares (first name unknown). I did know Simón Cruz, who had his own family. I remember meeting Olivares once. He worked at the courts in San Juan. This was all the information I could put together as a child. As an adult, I did not investigate my paternity any further.

During the years when the economic condition in my grandmother's house became critical, my mother decided that she and I would go to see Simón Cruz who, she said, was my father, at his place of work. On Saturdays, we would look for him. We would go to Miramar, an area of town where there were many beautiful homes. It was an exclusive section of Santurce. In Miramar, there was a foundry called Abarca, a big plant where they made machine parts and boilers from steel. A tall fence made of iron encircled the foundry. We would go to one of the tall gates to see the man who was supposed to be my father. We would watch for his assistant. My father was the driver of a large Mack truck. His assistant already knew us from our trips every Saturday. My mother would say that we had come to see Simón Cruz, and his assistant would look for him. I felt very bad, standing outside those gates looking for this man. When the man was found, he would come to the gates and speak with us through the railing. I always remember that his reception was cool and removed. It was obvious that he was not happy to see us. I remember his touching my head very reluctantly as my mother would ask me to say "Bendición, Papá (Bless me, Father)," and I would say it in a very low voice. He would answer, "Dios la bendiga (May God bless you)," and continue to talk with my mother. To this day, I hate these two expressions, although they are traditional greetings in our culture. This is the most contact that I remember with this man. He would say that he had a family and could not give us money. He would usually give us three dollars although my mother asked for ten. If we were lucky, we would get five dollars. Once we would leave the foundry, I would feel thoroughly humiliated and would walk very fast in front of my mother. This happened many times over many Saturdays until I finally told my mother that I would not go with her anymore. She explained that we needed the money to contribute to the home expenses and that we could not afford to be proud. I remember saying that I would never go again and that she could go alone. Later in my life, I put these experiences together with similar experiences related to the identification of my father.

I had a godmother who was a very popular person with her friends. She and my mother had been very good friends and had gone to parties together. My mother would tell me that I had to go to see her on Sundays. She lived in a very large house in the middle-class area of Santurce, called Ocean Park. Her house was very large and had a porch that encircled it, with many doors. I did not like to go because many children, who were also her godchildren, would be there. We would sit to eat, and Godmother would circulate through the rooms greeting everyone. Whenever I went, I would try not to be seen. I sat in a corner, and since I was a small girl, I could hide. I did not want to be seen because everyone was well dressed, and I wore faded hand-me-down dresses with shoes that had holes in the soles. My godmother was a loud, imposing figure, and I was afraid in her presence. I knew that she was a spiritualist, and people visited her for consultations during the week. One Sunday during my visit, I could not keep her from seeing me. I remember her saying, "Come here. Where is your mother? Why doesn't she come with you?" She spoke in a loud, thunderous voice. She continued, "Is she still taking you to see Simón? You tell her to come to see me. She has to stop doing that. That man is *not* your father. The man in the court, Olivares, is your father." As she was telling me this, I wished that the earth would open up and swallow me. As she turned her back, I rushed through one of the doors and left the house. Tears were pouring out of my eyes, blinding me as I walked up the hill from her house. I knew that I was not returning home. Instead, I walked and walked. I remember passing by my friend Blanca's house. Blanca and I had known each other because our mothers were friends. When I arrived at Blanca's house, her father's car was outside the house. I got in the car and cried. Blanca followed me into the car. We sat and I cried. I could not tell her what had happened. I felt too ashamed. I was happy that she never asked me the details of what had happened.

After this incident, I tried to remember if I knew this man, Olivares, who my godmother said was my father. I could remember an incident when my mother and I walked with a man, Olivares, in San Juan. He asked my mother, "Is this the little girl?" She said yes. He then caressed my head softly. While we walked, he took my hand. I never asked my mother any questions about this man. When we arrived at my grandmother's house, my mother reported that we had met a man called Olivares. This incident and my terrible experience with my godmother convinced me that I would never return to the foundry.

Seventy-seven years later when I returned to Puerto Rico to attend a meeting, my younger sister picked me up at the hotel to take me to the airport. We planned to meet hours early so that we could have a leisurely lunch and talk. During our lunch, we discussed our relationship with Mother. Haydée told me that she did not have a difficult relationship with Mother because she had always asked direct questions of her and did not allow her to escape from answering fully. My sister then proceeded to give me an example of this by telling me that she once asked mother who my father was and why she had left me with Grandmother. Mother told her that when she was a young woman, her mother would send her to deliver lunch to workers in an area of Santurce. There she met a young man with whom she fell in love. My mother was twenty-two years old. They both would meet after work in that area. One day, she found out she was pregnant and informed her lover. He told her his father had to approve of his marrying her. Mother told her father about being pregnant, and her father, after being furious, informed her that he was going to speak to the young man's father, whom he knew. My mother's father returned home ashamed and furious because the young man's father told him he would never permit his son to marry a black woman! The anger and the discussion of this event in the home resulted in my grandmother asking my mother to leave the house. My mother went to live with friends until she was ready to give birth. At that time, her mother admitted her into the house to have the baby, but when the baby was born, she asked my mother to go away and leave the baby. She could only see the baby a number of times during the day so that she could breastfeed her. One day, my mother secured a job, rented a room, and took the baby away when her mother was not there. Some weeks later, a neighbor where she rented the room came to my grandmother's house in search of someone who could get into Mother's room because the baby was alone inside and had been crying for hours. The neighbor said that several neighbors had tried to break the lock to find out what the matter was, but they were not successful. The neighbor decided to get someone from the family.

That night, my grandmother took the baby and would not allow Mother to see her again. My mother explained to Haydée that she had gone to a party and should have returned sooner, but became so involved in the dancing that she forgot about the time. She explained to my sister that she had always felt very guilty and very unhappy that this had happened with her baby. Later, in anger, she told her mother that if they did not let her see the baby, it was best because she did not want the baby anyway.

I was petrified to be talking about "the baby," who was me, over lunch. I remembered the stories that my mother would tell me and my half-siblings about the movie "Pinky" in which the light Negro rejects her black family. She said that Doña Carmen, the owner of the movie house, had said that I would do this to her, that I would reject her. I thought that this was a ridiculous idea. I realized, after hearing my sister's story, that our color differences may have always been an issue between us. I had been angry with my mother because she had abandoned me and had also not told me about my father. I now realized that my mother may have always considered I was rejecting her because of her color. I regretted that we had spent a lifetime misunderstanding each other.

I left Puerto Rico thinking about my mother with great pain, anger, and compassion. I regretted that I had never talked with Mother about this, and that we had never released one another of all the bad feelings. These memories bring back a situation that I have never resolved.

Growing Up Poor in Barrio Obrero

Our family was one of the many families that grew up poor in Puerto Rico, surrounded by a society where privilege, abundance, and opportunities existed for others. The families of Barrio Obrero, a workers' community, survived and enjoyed the benefits of a strong internal social structure of belonging and respecting one another. The struggles of living in this community, under these circumstances, affected me in both positive and negative ways. I was born in Puerta de Tierra, a slum of the Old San Juan city. San Juan is a walled city, and the wall had two doors: Puerta del Mar, which still exists, and the door to the land, Puerta de Tierra. These doors in the wall were made for people to escape in case an invader would win a battle and the inhabitants had to escape either by sea or by land. The land door does not exist anymore because the wall was demolished on that side as the city grew. Today, there is only a small piece of the wall where the door used to be. The people left behind as San Juan grew were poor families that rented railroad-type apartments in houses made of wood.

I must have been two or three years old when we left Puerta de Tierra and moved to Barrio Obrero. We were a poor family in a poor neighborhood. In Barrio Obrero, the streets were numbered from 1 to 17. Avenida Borinquen, the main avenue, had a plaza from streets 12 to 15. As you traveled away from Avenida Borinquen toward the water, called El Caño, the land became muddy, and when it rained, the waters flooded over the banks. The people who lived between Avenida Borinquen and Avenida A had sturdy houses. The first four houses were made of cement and the rest were made of wood. Houses below Avenida A did not have inside toilets or showers. They had outhouses. Barrio Obrero was built as a housing project for workers and their families who had lived in overcrowded areas. Other homes were built in the muddy areas by homeless, poorer people who had moved from rural areas.

Families living in Barrio Obrero did not pay rent. They paid taxes at the end of the year. This left us with the basic expenses of food, clothing, transportation, and medical care. In our family, we had a generous contributor to the food supply. We had a prolific breadfruit tree that fed us for years. You could add oil, vinegar, and codfish flakes to the breadfruit when there was money to buy luxuries. This tree was particularly important to us when Grandfather lost his job and after he died.

Barrio Obrero was a good neighborhood to grow up in. We all knew each other. There was a spirit of belonging, and we identified with one another. We knew of other neighborhoods, like Sunoco, but we always felt more united and proud of our own community. For other people, we were just a poor neighborhood, but we knew that we were more. Famous people were our neighbors. The Cortijos, a well-known family of musicians, lived in Barrio Obrero. Our neighbors were carpenters and cement workers who worked in the local factory.

Racial identity was not a major issue among the members of my neighborhood. We were a people of many colors and many shades. Some had straight hair; some had kinky hair, like mine; others had red or blond hair. This mixture was typical of the poor Puerto Rican neighborhoods. Although I would be considered a *grifra* (the name given to a person who has kinky hair, but has features associated with a Caucasian background), my mother was a black person with Negroid features, as were my grandmother and grandfather.

In the new home in Barrio Obrero, we had a place where we could have meetings. On some evenings, many men friends and coworkers of my grandfather would come to the house. They spoke loud, banged on the table, and used vulgar and dirty words and phrases. They were all workers who lived in the neighborhood. I would be put to bed and prohibited from coming to the parlor. However, I would get up and sit by the entrance of the living room to watch and listen. I was not allowed to participate or be seen. These men were angry at the tobacco factory owners. They wanted to get paid more money for their work. They wanted to form what was called a *sindicato,* a workers' union. My grandmother would bring coffee and large serving dishes full of *serenta,* slices of potatoes, tomatoes, *yautía, yuca,* avocado, rings of white onions, red sweet peppers, and sliced codfish. These ingredients were doused with olive oil, vinegar, black pepper, and oregano. The men ate, cursed, argued, and put forth proposals. In one of the meetings, they decided to strike. When they were leaving, one of the men said, "We have to watch out for the *rompehuelgas*" (strike-breakers). This small group needed to get other men to agree. The organizing would later escalate into activities that would cause great physical harm and economic disaster for my grandfather and his coworkers.

I remember many things about my grandmother that were negative and unpleasant. On the other hand, there were some things that I cherished. The new home in Barrio Obrero gave us an opportunity to share and have some pleasant experiences together. Every morning, Grandmother would wake up very early, before everyone else. Usually this was about five o'clock in the morning. She would fuss and putter in the kitchen to make *café colao* that filled the house with a wonderful aroma. *Café colao* is a very strong brew made by passing boiling water through a cotton drip bag of ground coffee—it is a very strong brew. At times, I would get up early and accompany her in her chores.

Our little house had a beautiful garden. On the right side we had flowering plants, and on the left side there were medicinal plants. My grandmother would walk in her small garden on the middle path that was covered by stones. She would carefully weed with the help of an old garden tool. As she tended each plant, she would tell me their names and explain their use. She would say, "This is *quinino*. It is good for a fever." "This is *gallito*. Its flowers can be made into a tea for a bad cold." On and on our rounds would go. As we passed each plant, I would absorb all the new knowledge, learning her love of flowers and plants, and enjoying these peaceful times with her. She always seemed most at peace, happy, and less distracted when she worked in the garden. A large white rosebush framed the porch of our wooden house. It always had an abundance of roses, very white with a tinge of pink in the middle. Our old dilapidated porch looked dressed up with the hanging bundles of roses. By the stairs, as you entered the house, Grandmother had a bush called *café de la India*. Further to the left, there were clusters of *nardos*. All of these flowers, plants, and trees smelled with a perfume that escaped once the sun had gone down. It was peaceful and enchanting to sit on our porch at night. The new house and my grandmother's garden allowed me to know another side of this strange woman who had such contrary ways of connecting with me.

I attended school in my neighborhood, on Calle 8, within walking distance from my home. I loved my neighborhood school from the very beginning. My aunt had taught me to read at home, so that when I entered a formal school, I was already advanced. I began school with a good sense of pride and accomplishment. We wore uniforms: a dark skirt and a white blouse with a yellow bow. Although the children who lived up from the plaza were better off economically than us, with our uniforms, it was not easy to distinguish us from them. During these early years of school, I felt very satisfied with myself.

Calle 14, the street where I grew up in Barrio Obrero, was right in the middle of Plaza Barceló. The children who lived on it played in the streets after dinner. I was permitted to go out and join the others in playing singing games, whose songs were old tunes from Spain. Sometimes the boys would play with us, but soon they would separate from the girls to go and play rough games. The street was not paved. We played in the sand. I remember how unhappy we all were when machines came from the municipality to replace the old sewer pipes and make trenches in the street. We were even more unhappy when they covered the trenches with gravel and tar and gave us a paved road with sidewalks on each side of the street. Now the games had to be different. From then on, I would ask permission to walk up the block to go and play in Plaza Barceló. You always had to ask permission whenever you intended to go further than the front of your house.

Going to the plaza, my friend Paquita and I realized that her sisters were already teenagers who could go to the plaza after dark and walk around the area, playing and flirting with the boys. A number of the younger children, including me, would play dirty tricks on them. For example, we found out that one of the boys had a car, which was almost unheard of in our neighborhood, and that he parked it on the side of the plaza. Barrio Obrero still had areas with cows in the middle of the city, and we decided to bring in cow manure from an empty lot, and put it on the seat of his car.

I was a very fastidious child and recognized at an early age, when I was about six, the circumstances of poverty and disorganization in my home after my grandfather's death. I reacted strongly to the disorder and did everything within my power to give myself a feeling of stability and confidence. I was very careful, in retrospect, even compulsive, about neatness and order. I remain this way today, although less compulsive. I took care of my clothing with great care. I made sure that I was clean and that my room was neat, despite the bareness of furnishings. I walked through the house with great care so as not to get hurt on the decrepit stoop or broken floorboards. To my neighbors, I became known as the "duchess," and at first I was ashamed of the mockery, but later I accepted it as a recognition of my difference. I internalized it as something positive, a part of who I would become.

I felt very different from the other children. I tried not to get dirty when I played, and since my grandmother forbade me taking off my shoes, I never walked barefooted. Every August, at the beginning of school, there would be pouring rains. My friends would walk home without shoes, hanging their shoes around their necks by the laces. We had a wonderful time walking into the streams of water running down the street. Everyone would do this except me. I wanted to play in this way, but I remembered that my grandmother warned me I would catch a cold and be out of school with asthma attacks. This was true. I remember having weeks of absences from school because I could not breathe at night and I would be exhausted in the morning. In those days, there was no medicine for asthma. My grandmother would hang raw garlic cloves around my neck so that the fumes would help my breathing. At night, she would drop a glob of Vicks vapor rub in boiling water, and I would breathe the fumes. After a few days, I would feel better and return to school.

I was skinny and not too athletic. I would stand on the sidelines when the rough games were played. All of this contributed to my concentrating at excelling in the more mental or intellectual activities. Even before formal schooling, I loved to read. However, this really meant that I did not engage in the natural childhood games and experiences that involved running, skipping, and jumping. In elementary and high schools, I avoided sports, gym classes, and anything that had to do with the use of my body in heavy physical exercises. I never went beyond the plaza until I was almost twelve years old. The children who lived on Calle 14 would go places together. On Saturday afternoons, we would walk about five to six blocks to the movie house for a matinee. We would only be permitted to go if we went together. I remember the movie house because that is where I saw the United States for the first time. Before the main movies started, we would always see a Laurel and Hardy short and a cartoon. I remember seeing movies by Diana Durbin, who sang beautiful songs, movies with Fred Astaire and Ginger Rogers dancing. I thought that the United States was a magical land so different from the world in which we lived! The stories would take place in big cities with tall buildings, lots of people hurrying about, and lots of cars. People lived one on top of another and went up and down in elevators. We could hardly believe that such a thing existed. The contrast to our way of life was so great because the houses in Barrio Obrero were very small, one story, and you entered by climbing only two or three steps.

When I was very small, my neighborhood was my whole world, except for Saturdays when I would be dressed by my aunt, who would take me to the bus on Avenida Borinquen. She would tell the bus driver to let me off in Parque Muñoz Rivera in Puerta de Tierra. I would always say to my aunt, "You do not need to tell him because I know where to get off." I would sit in the bus with my legs dangling from the seat, attentively waiting to get up before the driver told me. I would be very intent on letting him know that I knew where I was going. These were trips to meet my mother, who would be waiting at the bus stop. Muñoz Rivera Park was directly in front of the big factory building, the American Tobacco Company, where the entire family worked. I would be beside myself with excitement because I was going to meet my mother. When I arrived, she would help me off the bus. I would be very proud because she was saying to all the other women that I was her daughter Toñita. Everyone would comment to her that I looked very attractive. I always had a big bow in my hair. I thought that my mother was very beautiful, and I would walk with her, holding her hand, almost bouncing with joy. Years later, when I would feel so angry with her, I could never voice the good feelings and memories I had of her. Throughout all my years, the relationship with her would remain fixed with the anger of her not being available to me. However, on those Saturdays when we met, I remember her taking me to visit my great-grandmother, Doña Remigia, who was my grandfather's mother. Whenever we went to see this old lady, I would feel sorry and at the same time apprehensive because she was in bed and I understood that she was very sick. It was strange to me because this was an old white woman, the mother of my grandfather, and my grandfather was a black man.

As I mentioned earlier, after my grandfather lost his job, the family suffered from hunger and poor nutrition. There was a period, prior to his death, when food was available from the United States from an agency that distributed food and clothing. It was called "La PRA," the Puerto Rican Relief Administration. My grandfather would say that he was not going to take alms from anyone. Cheese, apples, and bacon were available, and my grandmother decided she would go to pick up the food for us. We had to learn how to cook and eat these foods.

Sometimes, I was invited to eat dinner when I went to study with my classmate Héctor Miranda, who lived up the street from us. At his house, we ate at a big table covered by a tablecloth that had beautiful needlework. The table was set for dinner with plates and silverware that matched. Each person had a cloth napkin, a side dish for bread, a glass of water, a plate, and a cup for coffee. The dining room had a beautiful hanging lamp in the middle of the room. Héctor's mother and aunt served soup from a large soup bowl. It was a ceremony in which we all engaged, and I liked it.

When I ate at this house, I had enough food, and often it was food that I had not eaten before. We ate potato croquettes, *chayotes* stuffed with meat, slices of fried plantain rolled and filled with ground meat, meat stuffed with ham, peppers, tomatoes, and onion, fried chickpeas with Spanish sausages, lentil or pumpkin soup. Above all, I had never eaten dessert in my home. At Héctor's home, dessert could be papaya in syrup, flan, candied milk, coconut candy, or candied orange with white cheese. The food in this house was always a dream for me, the poor kid from four houses down the street. Ever since dining at that house, I always wanted a home where the whole family would eat together at the table.

The desire for a middle-class life was born here at this time in my life. I aspired to own a house or an apartment with a dining room, a table covered with a tablecloth, matching dishes, and matching eating utensils. To me, these were my symbols of success and affluence. For many years, I lived in a house where everyone ate meals alone, sitting on the floor by the door of the kitchen, holding his or her plate with one hand and using a spoon to eat all foods. Each member of the household would eat when he or she arrived home. I would also eat next to my aunt Magui at the kitchen table. She would cut my meat or *panapen* in small pieces so I could eat it with my spoon.

I did, however, have memories of eating together at the kitchen table when Grandfather was alive. During those dinnertimes, I remember being told not to come to the table if I had not bathed or changed my clothes, not to put my elbows on the table, and instructed how to hold a fork and cut my meat. The instructions also included not singing while eating, not picking pieces of onion, pepper, or ham from the food (which I always did), not spilling food out of the plate on the table or on my clothes, and finally, not leaving the table before others had finished. These were the lessons taught by my grandfather and grandmother. I learned them all and felt very proud of doing these things and calling others down if they did not follow the rules. But after Grandfather died, all order collapsed. I felt unhappy and deprived.

It must have been from these early experiences that I learned order, ceremony, and rituals in my life. Aunt Magui contributed to the development of good habits by teaching me very early to brush my teeth, keep my shoes tied, and comb my hair. Much later, these early teachings would be integrated into the socialization of our first ASPI-RA students. The youths would attend fundraising dinners and teas with me. They had to learn how to eat at a table, and hold coffee and teacups while standing and talking to someone.

My Puerto Rican childhood was plagued with experiences of economic need and unfilled wants, but being poor did not take away from the self-respect that families were able to earn for themselves if there were qualities in you and your family that deserved that respect. Self-respect came from family name, being esteemed by others. Because none of us had money, self-respect was earned by qualities that were not associated with having money. For example, you could earn self-respect by being a courteous person who knew how to behave according to cultural expectations. You used the polite salutations and the proper exchanges between people. You respected the norms of behavior between people. If you were well behaved (*educado*), regardless of your money, dress, or position, you were respected.

The ravages of poverty became more influential in my life as I grew older. During the last years of junior high school, my home had generally deteriorated. There was no electricity, and I studied by a kerosene lamp during the evenings. The house was in disrepair. Part of it had collapsed when a supporting beam fell during a hurricane. The back door did not close well, and the three steps to the front porch were broken, and one was held in place by a stone. You had to be very careful when you came up the front porch.

Although the economic situation of my family was very bad, I insisted that I wanted to go to high school when I graduated from the eighth grade. For days, there were family discussions and arguments about my continuing school. It was my Uncle Conradito's opinion that I should go to high school because I was so small and skinny that no one would hire me. He felt that I might as well continue school and get a degree. Everyone felt that it was impossible because there was no money for the bus fare and my clothing was too poor to go out of Barrio Obrero to be with other young people. With my uncle's support, the decision was made to let me go to high school. I enrolled in Central High School, where most of the students were from families of better economic means than ours. The school was well respected, the only high school that we knew. I do not remember that I had any difficulty enrolling. Some other children from my area also attended the school. Once enrolled, I would walk daily from Barrio Obrero to Santurce with the other children who were going there. Today, such a walk would never be considered acceptable for children.

At Central High School, there was no chance but to associate with people whose names and incomes defined their importance and status.

Prior to this time, I had been protected by the dignity and status that my family had in Barrio Obrero. Now, thrown together with a different social group and social class, I no longer felt self-assured and confident. Here, social class was the major determinant of who you were and how you were treated and respected. During my high school days, I often spent evenings looking for hard cardboard to cover the holes in my shoes. I have never talked with anyone about these experiences. I remember getting a job in the high school cafeteria when there was no food at home for us to eat. I would take money home in my socks. When the purchaser did not need change, I would not go to the cash register. I would slip the money into my socks. This money provided food at home for the next day.

Poverty prevented me from attending school activities when I was in high school. Social dances were held in Escambron Beach Club, a very fancy nightclub near the beach. On significant holidays, the class would hold large dances with well-known orchestras. I could never attend because I did not have the proper dresses and shoes.

Throughout my four years of high school, I was very skinny and undernourished. My first year at Central High, I was pulled out of school and sent to a sanatorium in Aibonito. I had contracted tuberculosis. I lived in the sanatorium for three months. This was the year in Puerto Rico when the government led a campaign to discover and treat this disease among the island residents. Although it was difficult to be separated from one's family, there was no stigma attached to the disease because it affected people of all social classes. While living in the sanatorium, I received delicious fruits and food and lived in a sunny, comfortable environment with many other children.

In this respect, poverty had its advantages. I lived very well for the three months while my family had to live without these benefits. However, the disease left a legacy of poor health that I carried into my adult years.

I remember my unhappiness when I entered Central High School. I left my neighborhood behind and the feeling of belonging in Barrio Obrero. I wanted to sing in the Music Club, which put on dramatic singing and poetry recitals. My teacher in English class, Miss Del Toro, would never select me for these plays. I imagined it was because

I looked very bad in my ill-fitting clothes and my old shoes. From what I understood, only the rich children were selected. I remember going to the rehearsal room where they practiced. I have a very vivid memory of listening to the rehearsal of the *zarzuela, "La Ronda de los Enamorados." "¿Dónde estarán esos mozos, que a la cita no quieren venir . . ."* Sylvia Rexach participated in this club. She later became the lead singer in our school's large musical production performed at the Paramount Theater. To me, Sylvia looked like Ginger Rogers. Later on, when Sylvia became a famous composer and singer in New York City's Latin nightclubs, I would feel great sorrow to see that she had deteriorated into an alcoholic. People would pay for drinks for her as they requested songs.

Carmen Laguna was one of my best friends. She and I would play fantasy games to entertain ourselves during much of our time at Central High School. The games were built around the drawing of a map and hiding treasures throughout the yard of the high school. We envisioned ourselves as pirates who would discover these treasures. We had a secret code in which the map was drawn. Another girl involved in the game was Alice González. Alice lived in the upper part of Barrio Obrero, called Villa Palmeras. Carmen lived in Barrio Obrero also, but she lived in the entrance to the community, where teachers and professionals lived.

Alice and Carmen were both very shy, and in this threesome I was the leader. I had developed the game of pirates from readings about the pirate Cofrecí, a Puerto Rican who lived in southwest Puerto Rico. It was believed that his treasures were still in the waters off the coast.

Sometimes other youths would join us in playing. The treasures were stones, shells, and things that had interesting colors that could be considered jewels. Sometimes I would bring shells from my collection that I found during my trips to Cataño with my godfather when I was a child. As I look at these games with the eyes of an adult, it was a pretty childish game for high school students to play. However, the game occupied our time after school while we waited for the bus to take us back to our neighborhood. While we had no high social status in Central High, the game gave us some importance as it developed into our "secret society."

When Alice moved to the United States before finishing high school, she would write us long letters, many of which were written in the secret language that we had invented. Later, in my graduation high school yearbook, students wrote comments about the long letters that I received from Alice. I received much status from these letters because they were delivered by the postman and they came from the United States. I would read the letters as I stood in the hallways of the school waiting for my classes to begin. No one else but Carmen and I received the letters.

Vacations in an Enchanted Different World: Another Culture, Another Race

My summer trips to Loíza brought me into a completely different world. These were exciting times for me. I grew as a person in knowledge, values, and aspirations. My mother would arrange for me to spend a few weeks, during summer vacation, with my sisters and brother at the farm of her husband, my stepfather in Loíza. By the time I was nine years old, my mother had married Francisco López, the son of a landed family of Loíza. I would go with my brother Esteban to their farm to spend exciting and wonderful days. We would run around the farm, picking up sweet lemons, grapefruits, and oranges. We would run from behind the house, away from the main road, to the beach and play with other children from the area. All the children in Loíza had very dark complexions, and I would notice the differences between these children and the residents of Barrio Obrero, where there was a mixture of different colors in the people. The people in Loíza spoke Spanish with a different accent from ours. My brother Esteban and I would try to imitate them because we wanted to fit in.

At night, there were no lights on the road. Everything was very dark, and I enjoyed watching the stars. I was learning about the constellations in school, and would try to identify Orion. I told my brother that the stars were bodies very far away in the sky. We argued about whether God existed. He said that God lived up there, and I insisted that he did not. In our discussions about God, we concluded that God was everything, since he was supposed to be everywhere. During those summers, my brother and I became very close. We sang popular songs in harmony, and could sing for half a day without repeating a song.

My stepfather's mother, Doña Ricarda, was very stern and would correct us and try to curb our visits to the beach. Their home in Loíza had formal Spanish-style furniture, cane chairs, and rocking chairs with a sofa. They also had a dining area where we ate. They had a calf that would run from one end of the house through the front door to the back door. My stepgrandmother would get very upset because the calf would dirty the floor, knock furniture down, and make a mess of the house.

This was a house of much discipline. There were rules for helping with household chores. There were regulations for waking up in the morning, eating, and going to bed. These were rules of behavior, and I complied with them, so I never felt like an outsider. I was *la hija de Alejandrina*. Sometimes my stepfather was there with us. Sometimes he was not. I met my brother's aunts and uncles. They all had light complexions, as stepfather did. The family was well known in the area and they were treated with great respect. They had one of the only houses on the main road, and they had a farm that extended from the road to the beach. I think that the father of the family, during his life, had owned much land and had grown coconuts for sale. The food in this house was very different from the food in San Juan. We ate lots of fish and flat pancakes made of casave root flour, which we called *yuca*. We also ate *empanadas* made of *yuca* flour on the outside with crab-meat folded inside. These were cooked on hot stones. We ate *arepas de arroz* (riceflour pancakes) made on a hot stone also. This food and the style of cooking were from the Indians and the Africans. These experiences brought me in touch with people who were completely different from me and my other family. The people of Loíza had a culture that was very influential in my understanding that we Puerto Ricans had in us the Taíno, the original inhabitants of the Island, and the Africans, who were brought in as slaves. The inhabitants of Loíza were descendants of slaves who were given the land on the beach to live together. After their emancipation from slavery in Puerto Rico, they founded the town.

Although these differences were never directly discussed during my vacations in the countryside, Loíza brought this reality directly to me. Life in Loíza was very different from life in the city. There was lots of food. The air was very fresh and clean. There was a freedom to roam, play with animals, and visit the beach. People were very shy and lowered their heads when they spoke. As a child, I could never understand this behavior.

During my last summer there, I met a young man who drove a *público*, a type of taxi. I fell in love with him. I was fourteen. I would admire him from afar. I think that he felt a distance because he was a *público* driver, and my stepfather's family had a position of respect in the community. The young man never spoke to me, although he knew I wanted him to do so.

In June, there was always a celebration of San Patricio, the patron saint of the town. The image of the saint, carved in wood and kept in the church of the town, was taken out of the church and carried many miles away and returned to town three days later. There were ceremonies as the saint and the procession accompanying the saint were carried from place to place. There were ceremonial rituals of men on horseback who looked like Spaniards fighting with *vejigantes* who walked on stilts, with masks, who were said to represent demons. The *vejigantes* wore tunics and had pants of very bright colors. I thought the *vejigantes* were the black people. The ones on horseback, the Spaniards, would always win. The *vejigantes* would carry large bladders full of air. They made loud noises when people were hit. The *vejigantes* would hit people on the roads as they passed. Rhythmic chants were called out by the *vejigantes*, "*Vejigante está pintao*." The crowd would answer, "*De amarillo y colorao*." It was a time of great merriment, followed by a dance that was held in the plaza at the center of town, where I looked for the *público* driver. I never saw him again.

The evenings were most beautiful. The moon shone clear and bright through the trees. I never again experienced the calm and beauty of the absolute darkness of the nights. The close relationship with my brother during these summer vacations has lasted to this day. Unfortunately, these trips to Loíza lasted for only three summers.

In my adult years, I have returned to visit Puerto Rico and attended the Loíza Festival in June. I have not attended often because it makes me feel very sad. The festivities are now sponsored by beer, rum, and whisky companies. The older residents continue to hold the ceremonies, but they are held privately to preserve the meaning and to escape from the drunkenness and loud behavior of the mobs of people from other parts of the island and from the tourists who now attend. During this time, the town and the countryside are inundated with garish garlands of lights with ugly figures made of plastic similar to Halloween monsters, hanging from trees.

Establishing a Home and Becoming a Teacher

I have tried to identify experiences and problems of my childhood that shaped my personality. Some of these are now easy to remember, and I can trace them directly. They made me very proud and committed to self-sufficiency almost to a fault. Because I was brought up in a house of adults in which no one was responsible for me, I learned that I had to be in command of my own life. I had to invent my own ways, and I had to demonstrate to others that everything was all right with me. At a very early age, I learned to dress myself, to bathe myself, to eat, and to perform all the necessary acts that are usually done for a child by an adult. When my grandfather would teach me how to eat, I learned immediately how to use a fork, how to shift it from the right to the left hand without dropping food on the table or on myself.

Another significant and telling characteristic that I can remember is that when I would get hurt, I would go away for long periods of time. I would not let anyone know that I was hurt as I withdrew to a place where no one would be able to see me crying. I felt proud and did not want to let anyone know that I had been crying. I also remember that I had a need for someone to show me that he/she loved me and to have that person demonstrate it often and in many ways. This was the kind of demand that I would put on my Aunt Magui. Fortunately for me, my need matched her need to have a child to pamper.

As I grew older, I discovered that I had the ability to work intensely for long periods of time, in school and later, as a teacher. All these traits have been with me from the very early years of my childhood. Some are very positive and have helped me to achieve the success that I have enjoyed. Some of these have interfered and, to this day, cause me unhappiness.

One trait that has been crucial in my ability to solve problems and to move ahead decisively with assurance and strength is that I have little patience with indecisiveness. I am compelled to facilitate decisions and make people take action. The following set of events that occurred when I was about fifteen years old will illustrate one instance when I made a firm decision for the family that greatly changed the direction of our lives.

After I had spent nearly three months in the sanatorium recovering from tuberculosis, my Aunt Juanita asked my grandmother to let me come live with her. The reason that she gave for her request was that I needed to live in an environment where I would benefit from daily meals, have a clean and orderly house, and attend school with adequate electric lighting. She added that she was married to a man who supported the family comfortably and would gladly accept my entering his household.

Although my grandmother and aunt knew that I had some reservations, they accepted her offer because they did not want me to return to the situation that had caused my health problems. I went to live with Aunt Juanita, and I had my own room, plenty of food, and the best conditions for studying.

On weekends, my sisters Lydia, Ana Mercedes, and my brother Esteban would visit with my aunt's family and me. On one of these visits, Lydia, who was twelve years old, told us that my aunt's husband would make her sit next to him on the sofa and try to touch her genitals and rub her breasts. I became furious. My brother said that he would hit the man with a piece of wood that he kept under the house. I knew that he was a small boy and his attacks would be unsuccessful. I told him to wait, I would speak to our mother about an idea that I had.

The next day, I asked my mother to meet with me. I told her that children belonged with their parents, and I had been working on a plan to have us all live together. I said that I had applied for a job at the high school cafeteria in order to contribute to the expenses of our having our own home. I reminded her that she once had a business cooking and she could resume this activity to bring in additional income. I told my mother in a very firm and convincing way that we could succeed, so that she would not feel uncertain or fearful of the decision. That very day, I convinced her that we should look for a place to live. We located a house, and Mother signed the lease. By the end of the week, we had purchased furniture and moved into our new three-bedroom home. I was immensely happy because we had a dining-room table with a tablecloth where we could all eat together. We had matching dishes and silverware, and napkins. I helped my mother secure meal contracts with families in the area.

For the first time in my life, I lived with my mother. Her business did well. We continued to live in our new house on Calle Lippit near Barrio Obrero throughout my last years of high school and into my first years at the University of Puerto Rico. We lived on Calle Lippit until we moved into a public housing project, Caserío Las Casas.

I have always been the kind of person who had great determination, stamina, and a sense of planning for my life. I was always striving for better opportunities and chances for myself and those around me. The decision to attend the University of Puerto Rico depended upon my having enough money to pay for tuition. I did not have this money. Although tuition was very low, there were the other expenses of bus fare, books, and clothing. I needed decent clothing to be able to go into a place where there would be many young people from throughout the country who came from more privileged backgrounds.

My mother found a way to assist me in my ambition. Mother entered into a group called a *sociedad*. A *sociedad* is an economic cooperative transaction in which members pledge a weekly amount for twenty weeks. Each member selects a date when she or he receives all the money of the group. In the case of my mother's *sociedad*, she pledged to pay $10 weekly for twenty weeks. When it would be her turn to receive the money, school would be starting. She would receive $200, and I could buy clothing and have money to set aside for my daily bus travel. Mother continued in the *sociedad*, making payments for sixteen more weeks. For the first time, I saw my mother as a person concerned about me as her daughter. She was making sacrifices for me. I felt moved to express my gratefulness and recognition of her new concern about my well-being. She did not acknowledge my message, but I decided I would carry this new feeling with me. I felt that her contribution was very important to my future life. Her planning and sacrifices helped me toward my plans to obtain a university education. Even with her assistance, I still needed to find other sources of funds.

My friend Héctor's uncle, Luis Felipe Olmos, came to my aid. He was a librarian at the university library. He had met me many times at Héctor's home, where I would go to study and stay to eat dinner. Luis Felipe knew that I wanted to attend the university, and he also knew of my family's poverty. He decided that he would try to find out if there was financial aid for a poor student. He took important information about my family and said that he would let me know if he found any possibilities. Luis Felipe lived elsewhere and would drive to Barrio Obrero to have lunch at the home of his sister, Héctor's mother. One day, he came early and stopped at my house to talk with my mother about having found a scholarship that would be granted to a poor person. When I came home from school, he stayed to coach me on the interview that I would have with the head of a family that provided the funds. He said that he would be there to help me.

On the day of the interview, we drove to a house on Ponce de León Avenue. I remember the house very clearly to this day. It is still there and it is used by the YWCA. It is one of the historic houses of the area. We went up the steps—you entered the house from the second floor— and were received by a servant who brought us into the *ante sala*, a large receiving room. In the middle of the room, sitting on a beautiful rocking chair, was a very white woman with black hair made into a bow held by beautiful hairpins. She had on long gold earrings. Her blue eyes seemed cold. She never looked at me. Dressed in black, she could have been a member of Spanish nobility. Luis Felipe introduced me, but she would not give me the benefit of a glance. She said to him that she had read about my family's poverty and where we lived, but she wanted him to tell her if I was deserving of the help that she would offer. He tried to include me in the answers he gave, but she finally turned the rocker in such a way that she did not have to see me. I grew angry and felt the heat on my ears. She gave the check to Luis Felipe and called the servant to show us out.

Luis Felipe said, "I am sorry that this happened this way. I had rehearsed with you because I thought that the interview would have been done with you. I hope that you do not feel too bad. We got the scholarship check, anyway. That is the important thing."

I did not say anything to him, but knew that he knew that I was very upset. We drove back to Barrio Obrero. I thanked him for his help. When I went into the house, I went to Aunt Magui, who held me while I sobbed as I told her what had happened. She said, "You are going to the university. One day that woman may know that you succeeded. I want you to wash your face, put the check away, and get your mind ready for your studies."

Throughout my early life, I had to deal with great poverty and lack of resources. Because of my fierce determination and tenacity, I have been able to achieve in spite of the impositions of class structures that exist in my country.

My time at the University of Puerto Rico was full of discoveries. I was excited about a course in economics, another in art and design. During the two semesters of English literature, I fell in love with that language and its poetry. I have to admit that this love was because of my English professor, Mr. Frederick Sackett. He taught me to love the poetry of Byron, Shelley, and Yeats. I began to try writing in English. Much later in my life, as I began to develop a clear political consciousness, I would question my childhood love of the English classes and my dates with Americans during the war years.

I left the university before the end of the required two years of the normal school diploma, to replace a teacher who was leaving for the army. Those of us who took this step to begin early teaching were given credit toward our diploma.

With my new income, we moved to a low-income housing project that was new and attractive. My stepfather, Francisco, would come to our new home during the week while I lived and worked at my country teaching assignment. My arguments with my mother about his presence in the house became open and harsh because I believed that Francisco received special privileges from the women of the house. He did not contribute to the expenses of the home. My mother responded with fury and demanded that I treat "the man of the house with respect." I replied that I paid the bills for everything and that he had no rights in the house. The situation between mother and me deteriorated over the years as we continuously argued about his presence in the house. My sisters and brother were be terrified by the arguments. They would hide in the back rooms. After all, Francisco was their father.

I had constant debts because I was carrying all the responsibilities. Mother had closed her business once we moved to the Las Casas housing project, and she got pregnant again and added another child to be supported. I was teaching in a rural area and returning on weekends.

As I now look back on my first teaching experience up in the mountains of Puerto Rico, I find it incredible that I was able to accomplish my goal. My first teaching experience was in a rural school in Cuchilla. It was vastly different from anything I had known. Our school was a long wooden house with two doors. On the opposite walls, there was a large chalkboard. The children sat on long wooden benches around three tables. At the table to the right of my desk sat six children who attended the first grade. At the middle table sat seven children in the second grade, and at the table to my left sat eight children in the third grade. I invented a schedule to teach each group while the other two groups engaged in art projects or silent reading under the leadership of a monitor selected from the older children.

As I became more comfortable in my responsibilities with the students, I found that the parents saw me as a person to whom they could bring their problems. They began coming to me after school to request counseling and advice. I was very young and lacking in life experiences, but I found myself growing up fast by trying to provide answers to problems I had never experienced. One day, a parent who had been described by other parents as a person "who chewed knives" came to see me. I found him to be an intelligent person seriously committed to the well-being of the children. He explained that his visit was to inform me that an English inspector came to the school every year to evaluate how well the teacher was teaching English to the children. He offered to help me prepare for the inspector by giving me a warning prior to the evaluation visit. He explained that he would be informed in advance of the inspector's arrival because he had a friend who worked in the town. His friend would come up the hill with the news in time for me to prepare the children for the visit. He added that parents did not think that learning English was as important as learning to read, write, and do arithmetic in the language of their country. I said that I needed his help as I prepared for the inspector. The children and I prepared a drama in which the children who were the fastest learners would phonetically learn words from the teaching guide, and I would call on them to answer during the inspector's visit. We rehearsed and got ready for the visit.

Some time later, the messenger came to inform us that the inspector had arrived in town and was hiring a horse to come up to the school. When the inspector arrived, the children and I were ready and played the small drama that we had planned. The visit went very well. I received a high evaluation. The inspector left, and the parents came in to find out how the evaluation had gone. The message of our success with the English inspector had reached all the parents, who then came to the school to hold a party. At the party, we all developed a very close and warm relationship. After this incident, every Friday when I left the mountains to return to my home for the weekend, my horse would move very slowly because the children would hold on to his tail. I always left with my arms full of gardenias, pineapples, and oranges. I would hear their voices saying, "*Maestra, ¿regresará el domingo?*" I would answer, "*Sí, volveré.*" This period of teaching in the mountains was a most unforgettable experience that helped me to become who I am.

My second teaching appointment lasted for one year. It was an experimental program in what would today be called an innovative project. We had the freedom of teaching with new approaches and methodologies. I was given freedom to invent different methods, using my imagination and knowledge of children to make classes interesting and exciting for the children. I had been recruited for this assignment. Our school, La Segunda Unidad de Padilla, was known as one of several model schools established on the island in the hills of Corozal and other rural areas. The children were close to my own age, and I communicated well with them. I enjoyed this work during the week, but when I came home on the weekends, my life continued full of tension and arguments with my mother. I worried about the bills that were always paid late. Sometimes, because of the economic conditions on the island, I did not receive my teaching salary for three months. I had to buy food, uniforms for my sisters and brother, pay installments on the furniture, and pay rent. To supplement the household income, Mother made candy that my brother would sell in the neighborhood movie house. We returned to receiving secondhand clothing and food from the homes of friends. I had no one to talk to about these conditions and my feelings. When I came home on weekends, I would stay locked in my bedroom or used the time to clean the house with the help of my brother and sisters. One activity that they loved was to watch me as I drew the view from my window. We lived on the second floor. From my window, I could see the silhouette of the three peaks of the mountains of the rain forest, El Yunque. While I drew, I would tell them stories about the Taíno Indians and their beliefs that two gods—Yukiyú, the god of good, and Huracán, the god of evil—lived in the mountains. This was one of the legends of our aboriginal ancestors in Puerto Rico.

The War Years in Puerto Rico—1942–1944

While I was going through my own personal, tumultuous problems, Puerto Rico had entered into the middle of the United States' Second World War. The United States had entered the war, but to Puerto Ricans this event did not make much of a difference until new realities brought this directly to us. Our young men were drafted into the armed forces, and we heard the news of submarines in the waters of the Atlantic Ocean. The availability of food and other products was also interrupted. These circumstances drove home the knowledge that we were a colony. There were arguments by our political advocates for independence that we did not belong in this war. Since large corporations benefiting from commerce with the United States controlled the media, we were never given a full discussion of the pros and cons of our participation in the war. However, the discussions continued at the neighborhood level, and we could not understand why our young men had to go to war. I did not have enough knowledge to make a rational decision on this matter, but I was affected by the anti-American sentiment that was prevalent throughout the island.

During the war years, food became scarce. Ships were not bringing food from the outside. Since we had stopped growing our own food, there was a very serious shortage. Puerto Rico was full of American and Puerto Rican soldiers and sailors. The army and the navy set up entities called United Service Organizations (USO). Older women who had a social position of respect were asked to get young girls to entertain the soldiers and sailors in their homes. Most of the women were middle-class white women and wives of businessmen. A black woman, Rosita Colón, who was very well-known because of her hairdresser shop, was one of the few black hostesses to organize activities for black American enlisted men. Her shop and her home were located in Barrio Obrero, Calle 4, where people of a certain higher status lived. Rosita hosted activities in her home and asked me to attend. I knew her because she was my beautician and I would go to the movies with her son.

Most of the American servicemen were about eighteen to twenty-one years old. I was amazed at how young they were. During the social events, we danced and talked with the young men, who were fascinated by the Puerto Rican girls. One sailor from Pittsburgh was enamored of me because he considered me "so refined and so petite." On our second evening, he asked me to marry him before he went to the war front. Of course, I answered no. We knew that the servicemen were stationed on the island temporarily on their way to Japan and Europe, so we did not consider their proposals seriously.

Discussions with the American enlisted men were very shallow. Never was there any mention of war. Language made it almost impossible to communicate well, but we knew that they were enthralled by us. A few of the girls married American sailors. My friend Blanca was going out with an American sailor, whom she later married. A strong wave of complaints from Puerto Rican soldiers emerged in the local newspapers about "our girls" going out with the Americans. The relationships of Puerto Rican women with American sailors were looked upon very negatively, almost like the relationships men had with prostitutes. This was said because the men congregated at the docks, where many prostitutes lingered. There were many reports in the press of Puerto Rican soldiers beating up the American enlisted men and women who accompanied them.

While walking on Muñoz Rivera Park, I met a young white soldier from Fayetteville, North Carolina. We would meet on weekends at the park. Sometimes we would go to the movies. He would bring rations and surplus food to my family. As a matter of fact, he visited the *residencial* (public housing project) where I lived with my family. We wrote one another when he went to the war front in Europe. He seemed to be very lonely and sad. He drank a lot of beer alone, since I did not drink. He did not have any friends in his group. The other men seemed to be from New York and New Jersey.

These were casual relationships that lasted a very short time as the servicemen were constantly disappearing. I always thought that these USO socials were for Americans. They were not held for the Puerto Rican servicemen. On one occasion, I went with a group of mothers and young women to visit their family men in Camp Tortuguero, where Puerto Ricans were stationed. There I met Ismael Zayas, a soldier from Ponce who began to visit me at my grandmother's house. He would bring different foods to my grandmother, who liked Ismael. She would often say that he was a good prospect for a husband. He was very fair, with a big mop of red hair. I used to say to her, "If you think Ismael is such a good catch, why don't you marry him?" She would laugh.

We learned that there were submarines off our shores and that this was the reason that merchant ships could not bring food to the island. The newspapers carried accounts of our lack of food. The blame for this situation was placed on our farmers, who had abandoned their farms and moved to the cities and to the United States. This was the level and nature of the political discussion in which the general public was engaged.

Teaching and My Departure from Puerto Rico

I continued my teaching, but I had been moved from the experimental school to a junior high school in Toa Alta. I had enjoyed working in the experimental school, but I was moved with the explanation that the new school would be closer to my home, thereby eliminating the travel and boarding expenses that I had. In spite of this explanation, I knew that the Padilla school position had become a choice assignment and that these positions generally went to relatives of superintendents and principals. The junior high school was in an urban location, and I soon saw that there was a great difference in the practices and methods of teaching in urban and metropolitan schools. In my rural school, the teachers were very connected to the children and their families. Padilla had been an innovative school with much discussion of the students' learning needs and our teaching approaches. The atmosphere in Toa Alta was different in that teachers did not share ideas. Everyone left the school grounds immediately at the close of the working day, and there was no professional or social interaction as colleagues.

Teaching in the new setting only complicated the problems of my home life. I was so overburdened, carrying the major financial responsibility for the family. I was suffocating with emotions and responsibilities. I needed to find my own life. I felt that the culture was oppressive, demanding that I take care of my mother's family because I was unmarried. Although my mother's husband lived with her during the week, he continued to live in his primary home with his mother in Loíza on weekends. Because he had lost an arm and was considered disabled, it was not easy for him to secure employment. Nonetheless, I resented his presence in the home without contributing financially to the care of his children.

Because of these problems, I fell into a serious state of depression. These were agonizing days for me. I finally spoke with my friend Cucha who lived across the street. She suggested that I speak to her minister whom she considered wise and understanding. She reminded me that I had met him when she wanted me to join her church. To my dismay, I recalled that when I had previously met Father Falcón, I had plagued him with questions as to why people needed religion, about the violation of one's self-respect by the requirement for adoration and submission to a god, about the virgin birth of Mary. The reverend had been very patient with me in my impertinence and naive attacks. Although I felt ashamed of my past behavior with him, I agreed to see him and request his help.

Consulting Reverend Falcón was a good decision. I asked him to help me find peace in my life. He helped me greatly without telling me what to do. He asked questions that helped me to identify clearly what was, in reality, my responsibility to my mother and her children. I almost felt that he was giving me the permission that I needed to leave by asking me such questions as, "Are you the father of those children? Are you your mother's husband? What makes you think that they cannot find the solutions to their problems if you are not here? Isn't it arrogant to think that one is indispensable?" He also added, "Wanting to leave seems reasonable. Leave the island, but do it in a responsible way. Show care and love for those that you are leaving behind. Do not create bigger problems for yourself. Others have left their homeland before. I came from Spain, across the ocean, to Puerto Rico. Now you must promise me that you will be careful with that feverish imagination and with your search for logical answers for every question. Go, and write me once you are there."

Second Part

I Take a Leap Over the Sea and I Land on My Feet (1944–1949)

The Trip Across the Ocean into a Frightening World

The city of New York had always been an enchanted world for me—part reality and part dream. I knew the city as the place where my mother and her brothers had gone to visit. Although I had been told that the trip ended abruptly because of my uncle's illness, the city always remained a fairy place in my mind, derived from stories of returnees and movies.

My mother was about nineteen when she traveled to New York. We rarely talked about the trip. There was never much time for talking together. I learned about this trip from Aunt Magui, who remembered when they left. She said that my mother had been very courageous to leave Puerto Rico. They lived in the city on Amsterdam Avenue at 120th Street with Victoria, the sister of Rafael Hernández, the composer. Their stay was not too long because my uncle, José Belén, had gone partying without a coat and caught pneumonia. This forced the three to return to Puerto Rico with Uncle José. He died of pneumonia following their return. This seemed to be one of the things that my grandmother held against my mother. I thought that I could go to New York one day the way they had.

When this adventure was spoken of at home, my aunt referred to a steamer called the "Carolina." In the living room of our small house, there was a big steamer trunk where my grandmother kept presents that were given to her. It had been part of the luggage that they had used for the trip. The trunk held my grandmother's treasures, but it was a symbol of faraway lands for me. In the trunk, Grandmother packed her most valuable objects: the black shawl imported from Seville that was embroidered with luscious red, pink, and yellow roses; fans made of bone, encrusted with colorful stones; and a set of Spanish playing cards that no one ever used. Whenever Grandmother opened the trunk to store a new present that would never be used, I would hurry to take a peek at her collection of treasures. In my mind, the trunk, with its treasures, belonged to the same world where New York existed.

I was very young when I first heard the stories of my mother's trip. On Saturday afternoons, when visitors sat in the living room and talked, I would sit and listen to the stories of my mother, who was described as the courageous woman who had taken the trip. To myself, I would think that she should not have returned to Puerto Rico. I assumed that my mother had learned to speak English, although she pretended that she had not. I imagined that she must have lived an exciting life in New York. Like many others, I thought that land outside Puerto Rico was almost magical.

Everyone in Puerto Rico had a relative or knew someone who had gone to New York. Our next-door neighbors, the Encarnación family, had a son who had visited his family after moving to New York City. His name was Monchín. I had seen many photographs of Monchín on the roof of his building in New York. I had met Monchín when he was twenty. He had returned to our community dressed in a double-breasted coat with a felt hat and black, pointed shoes. He looked handsome and elegant, but I thought that he was showing off by wearing such a coat to Puerto Rico. He had impressed us all. I thought that I would like to wear such a coat when I grew up. I concluded that winter clothes were more elegant than summer clothes. I still believe this. This early impression was confirmed by the many movies that I saw. I would always look forward to going to the movies on the weekends because I could see scenes of New York. I always thought these must be the experiences that my mother had during her brief stay in New York. It never occurred to me that life was anything but glamorous and elegant in this city far away. I remember seeing the Ziegfeld Follies with Ruby Keeler. I loved the movies of Fred Astaire and Ginger Rogers.

I was looking forward to New York. I had great expectations of seeing movies, wearing different clothing, and living the life that I had fantasized about all those years. I looked forward to arriving in the port where I would see the Statue of Liberty. My friend Carmen Laguna, who was also a teacher, had decided to go to New York with me. It never occurred to me or to Carmen to live in any place other than New York City.

I awaited my new life in a new country. I was full of excitement.

The morning that we left for the United States, my mother embraced me. The year was 1944. I think that this was the first time that I could remember that my mother kissed me or showed any affection toward me. I felt wonderful, and I cried.

As I looked from the deck of the departing ship at my brother and sisters, I thought that I would never see them again.

As soon as the ship was launched, Carmen became terribly ill. We had remained on deck to get the last view of the island as it disappeared from our view. When we both started on our way to our room, Carmen felt dizzy and nauseous. She could not walk straight. With my help, we made it to the floor below. In spite of the recommendation from other passengers and soldiers that she should stay on the deck to get fresh air and not give in to her dizziness, she went to bed and only got up to eat soup, drink soda water, and go to the bathroom. I, however, went in and out, swaying back and forth.

I made friends with other passengers and the soldiers. I found two young men who had gone to Central High School with Carmen and me. Julio and Reinaldo would become our friends and companions for the trip. There were about two hundred American soldiers and fifty civilians aboard. We learned from the soldiers that our ship was one of the convoys that traveled from Puerto Rico to Guantánamo, Cuba. They also informed us that the highly visible dark spots on the water were oil slicks from ships that had been sunk by German submarines that were very active in these waters. Much to my amazement, I did not feel any fear about our safety during the trip. Exploring the ship and talking with the soldiers, I learned that a large portion of our ship carried war equipment. I also noticed that we always had one ship in front of us and one behind us.

In Guantánamo, other cargo ships and an air blimp joined us. After leaving Cuba, we faced bad weather. One day after breakfast, we received life jackets to wear when going on the deck. I went up to the deck that day, but I was asked to return to the stateroom when enormous waves made the ship look like a small toy about to be swallowed by a monster. I was very much afraid, but in a way I felt very exhilarated to be experiencing events that would never have been possible on the island.

The friendship with the soldiers provided us with a constant source of information about locations that we were passing and where we would eventually dock. One of the soldiers, a black man, brought Carmen and me a gift that he called a ration K dinner kit. He explained that the box was given to soldiers when they were on maneuvers for several days. The kit consisted of a number of cookies and bars of chocolate that we were told had enough nutrition for surviving several days if food was not available. After tasting one of the chocolates, Carmen and I put them away because they were tasteless. Little did we know that these ration K kits would be very important during the latter part of our trip.

On the dawn of November 19, the passengers were awakened and prepared for landing. That morning at seven o'clock, my life in the United States began. After being received by an army band that played "I'll be loving you always . . ." and thick fog that obscured the fact that the ship had traveled up the Mississippi River, I began to realize that we were not entering New York City. We were in New Orleans!

The arrival in the South was an experience for which none of us was prepared. None of us had any idea about racism as practiced in this country. Julio was a black man. I am what in Puerto Rico is called a *grifa* (a light-skinned person with kinky hair). Reinaldo was a white man with reddish hair, while Carmen was a white-complexioned woman with wavy black hair and thick lips and nose. This combination of color and facial characteristics was to cause many difficulties for us. Although in Puerto Rico we knew that race was a source of problems, we were never denied entry or were separated by race.

Army buses transported all passengers to the train station on Canal Street in the city of New Orleans. We lost our identity as passengers on the navy transport ship, and we became vulnerable because we could not speak English well. We did not have any sense of how to get where we were going. The men who were with us tried to speak English and ask about our train tickets to New York. Everyone spoke so fast and was so impatient with us that it was impossible to get clear answers to our questions. Each of us tried with no luck. Finally, an old black man came to our assistance. He was a porter in the station. He showed us the window where we were to buy the tickets for the train to New York City. He also told us the gate and number of the train that we needed and indicated the boarding time. We were very grateful for his help, but before we could express our thanks, he had left. The train bound for New York was leaving in the early evening. We had arrived early in the morning, so we had a whole day to wait. After checking our luggage in a wall locker, we decided to go and see the city.

Canal is a very busy business street, and we figured that we would not get lost if we did not stray from it. Because we had not had breakfast or lunch, we stopped in a small coffee shop to eat. The place was very busy. One of the fellows went to the counter to place our order, and we stayed behind him. The man and woman serving behind the counter took everyone else's order, but they would not take ours.

The man said to the woman, "They are foreigners." She answered angrily, "They are Niggers."

They both spoke with an accent that we could not understand very well, but the message came through that we were not going to be served. We concluded that we posed a problem for them, and we left.

Outside in the street, we felt discouraged, and after talking it over, we decided to return in the direction of the train station. We passed a fruit stand, where we bought a bag full of fruits and potato chips. Nearby, we found a movie house, and one of us suggested going in, since the movie showing was Eugene O'Neil's, *The Hairy Ape*. We did not notice that we were ushered to the second floor. After the movie ended, we returned to the station where we ate our cookies and chocolate bars from the ration K kit. This became our food for the day.

When our train was announced, we approached the gate where there was a mob of people boarding. A black porter called out, "Niggers in the back." Here was the problem again. It became evident that Negroes had a negative position. We did not know why they used the word "Nigger." It was confusing that the people sending Negroes to the back were Negroes themselves.

In the bedlam of boarding, Julio and Reinaldo stayed behind us saying, "You sit on the last seat of the white car, and we will sit on the front seat of the black car. Don't move, no matter what. We will be watching you." And so we did.

There were soldiers, sailors, and all kinds of armed forces personnel with their duffel bags. The aisles were completely filled with baggage. Unfortunately, the last seat of the car did not recline, so we spent a three-day trip sleeping in straight-back chairs. We ate whatever vendors would sell us through the windows as the train made many stops in local towns. It seemed as though we were stopping at every small station. One soldier called the train a milk train. We passed houses that were made of wood, cardboard, rags, and other improvised materials. Kids in ragged clothing sold apples, Coca Cola, and doughnuts as we passed their stations. All the children were black. As the hours passed, my heart was sinking for fear that we had committed a mistake. If this was the United States, *we had made a terrible mistake.* I kept reminding myself that this was not New York and I should hold my judgment until we reached the city.

During those difficult days and nights of the train ride, I reviewed the incident in the cafeteria where we were not served, the movie balcony, and the porter calling "Niggers in the back." I began to understand that "Nigger" was a negative term for Negroes. It began to feel like the raping of our innocence. This was the United States of America, and we four Puerto Ricans were being initiated into U.S. racism.

The arrival in New York City at night through a tunnel began the process of chipping away at the romantic dream of arriving in the port with the Statue of Liberty greeting us. Instead, we were introduced to the colonial experience, in the belly of the beast, through the tunnel into Pennsylvania Station.

Arriving in New York City

The arrival in New York was frightening. We had not only been robbed of the thrill of seeing the Statue of Liberty, but no one was present to greet us. Since our friends were picked up by their relatives, Carmen and I found ourselves in an immediate problem. The platform was emptying and we were almost alone. Everyone was rushing to a moving electric stair. I said to Carmen that we should watch how others moved and how they got on the stairs. We had never seen anything like an escalator. I was talking to Carmen, but I was really talking to myself. I watched and discovered that you placed one foot first and then you had to place the second foot on the stair so as not to fall. The next problem was how to get off, but I soon discovered that the stairs actually pushed you out, once you reached the top. As we approached the top floor, I could see a very beautiful ceiling with many designs. I said to Carmen, "There is a very high, beautiful dome, but do not look up now. If you do, people will think that we are hicks." Of course, people could see from our cotton clothing and our pitiful suitcases that we were hicks, but this never occurred to me.

Since no one was waiting for us, we found our way to a taxi stand and announced to the driver that we needed to go to the corner of Beck Street and "Avenue St. John" in the Bronx. I used my best English pronunciation, and the driver understood! We left the city by crossing a bridge and continued on our journey. The driver knew that we were nervous, and he told us that we were almost there. We took our suitcases, paid the driver, and continued to the building where Alice lived. The door had a beautiful lace curtain covering the glass. We rang the bell, and a woman came to the door and asked us if we were the girlfriends of the Filipino woman. We were told that Alice had gone to the train station to meet us.

The room where we sat to wait for Alice was very dark, lighted only by candles, with a large dining room table. The candelabra was highly polished and made of brass. The woman gave us towels and directed us to the bathroom, saying that we probably wanted to wash our faces. As we looked at ourselves in the mirror, it was true that our faces, hands, and clothing were dirty. We were served apples, milk, and crackers with butter that had no taste. We were very hungry, so we ate it all. When Alice returned, we climbed up to her fourth-floor apartment. Once there, she explained that on Fridays, the Jewish people did not use the electricity and that their butter and crackers were made without salt. She appreciated her neighbors meeting and greeting us. I will always remember with warm feelings being welcomed to New York by Alice's Jewish neighbors, even if the woman thought that Alice was Filipino.

I was very unhappy my first weeks in New York City. I felt that my heart was breaking. I cried every night without letting anyone know. I was convinced that coming to New York had been a mistake, and I just knew that I would not make a successful life in the city. I had several experiences that confirmed my feelings. I found that I could not perform the simple task of shopping for food, since people did not understand me.

It was becoming very cold, and the only warm clothing that I had was my white suit that I had made for the trip. The white cotton suit identified me as a newcomer. In those days, people coming from Puerto Rico usually came in a ship called the *Marine Tiger.* Even though I had come by the *SS Florida,* young people made fun of me when I walked on the streets, shouting "Marine Tiger," meaning to hurt and ridicule me. My crying and feelings of defeat stopped after one evening when I could not sleep. I stood at the window for a long time saying to myself, *I will learn the language, learn how to travel by myself, buy new clothing, and become a New Yorker! I know that I can. I must and I will!*

A week after we arrived in New York, Alice, her father, and her sister said that Carmen and I needed to have warm clothing. The decision was made by them that we would go with Alice to pick out coats that her father was purchasing for us as gifts. Alice gave me a sweater that she did not use and another to Carmen. Wearing the sweaters, we went down to Manhattan to shop for winter coats.

This was our first trip out of the new neighborhood since we had arrived from Puerto Rico. I was very excited because I thought that the Bronx, where we lived, was ugly. We traveled by the Third Avenue elevated train so that we could see parts of the city from above. We traveled to 14th Street, where we expected to purchase a coat for a good price, at Klein's Department Store, where there were many choices and prices from which to select.

Traveling on the train as we moved downtown, through the windows you could see into the homes of people, who would wave to us as we passed by. Children sat on windowsills and said hello as we passed. The train was a dark vehicle and made lots of noise. Soon Alice let us know that we had left the Bronx and we were in Manhattan, where I could already see the difference. The buildings were taller and people moved in a much faster way.

In front of Klein's, there was a park, Union Square, that I thought was the most beautiful park I had ever seen. Klein's and Orbach's, the two stores that I remember clearly, no longer exist. Union Square would become very significant in my education into the city. I could not stop from marveling at all the political speakers who would address crowds there. I did not understand fully the messages of the speakers, but I was fascinated by the activity and the spirit of the small group interactions. Years later, I would return to Union Square to hear the messages of many speakers on the fraud of the Consolidated Edison Electric Company, the assassination of Trotsky in Mexico, the strength of the proletariats of the world overthrowing the bourgeoisie, and the calls to salvation for those who would repent.

Employment in the City

My first job in the city was in a factory. Alice's sister, Guillermina, had taken charge and instructed us in how to find jobs. She took off from her job and went out early with us one morning, and by the afternoon we both had jobs. We had searched the newspaper and selected the best opportunities. Guillermina had negotiated the jobs and made sure we would begin the following day. It was easy to find work, for these were the days of World War II and the jobs were plentiful. I began by earning almost double my salary as a teacher in Puerto Rico. The job consisted of attaching small colored wires to parts of the chassis of radios for submarines. I would earn $125 a week. I had a job, but I had no life. The job took all my energy, and traveling back and forth to work consumed all my waking hours.

At my job, we all worked on a long assembly-line table. I was the third person at the table. I attached the small wires to the radio chassis with pliers and then soldered the wires with a hot soldering iron and a roll of wire. The tower of the chassis would grow tall, and other towers would pile up in front of me because I was so slow. The foreman would come to me and ask me to work faster. I would get very nervous. We worked from early morning until 10:00 P.M., with a half hour for lunch and a half hour for dinner. By quitting time, my arms would be weak from exhaustion and my fingers trembled. I had never done such hard work. Although Alice had tried to teach me how to relax by placing myself in a tub of hot water and salts, my hands were so tired that I could hardly hold a pen to write.

One day I dropped the hot iron from my hand onto my finger and it caused a serious burn. The foreman cursed, raved, and ranted. He called me "accident prone" and took me to the nurse. After my finger was swabbed with some yellow medicine and wrapped in a bandage, my arm was placed in a sling, and I went home. I returned to work the next day, and the foreman placed me in another job. This time I had to insert tubes in the radio chassis according to a chart placed in front of me. This was an improvement in my assignment, since I had no assembly-line pressure. I now sat on a chair in front of a small table that faced the two elevators in the entrance hall. Several days later, two young women came to be interviewed. I could see them as they were waiting for the elevator. One of them leaned against the elevator door. The door collapsed in, and she fell down the shaft, screaming all the way down. Everyone in the factory was in hysterics. I felt so bad that they had to take me into the restroom to calm down.

The next day I did not return to work. I followed the job-searching process that I had learned from Guillermina, and two weeks later I had another job. This time I found out that one could apply for a job with the federal government by filling out an application and taking a test. I completed these steps and I was accepted as a clerk. I worked in a very large room with others in rows of desks that held envelopes filled with coupons for gasoline, sugar, auto tires, and various food and clothing items. These coupons were rations for scarce items. The office was called the Office of Price Administration. I worked there until the war ended in Europe.

In addition to the fact that I earned much less money in the new job, there were other conditions in the Office of Price Administration that were not as much fun as in the factory. The workers in the factory were from Italy, Poland, and some from Ireland. The Italians all liked me very much and set out to teach me English. The day the first snow fell, they had lifted me up so that I could see the snow falling on an old cemetery that you could see through the window. There was always great merrymaking with jokes and singing. Much to my consternation, the men in the factory would stick their hands into the women's behinds, and the women would grab their penises. They would tell jokes that I never understood. They brought food from home and they shared with one another. It was like a big family.

In the Office of Price Administration, there was very little talking during work time. The little merriment was among the Italians and the Jews, not across the groups, but within each group. There were a large number of both Italians and Jews. There were about three Puerto Ricans, but they did not speak to one another. Only one black woman and a group of three Italian young women befriended me. I made a relationship with an Italian man who worked in the mail room, and we met after work. He had a thick accent and had just arrived from Italy. His name was Belluci.

When rumors began that the war in Europe would soon end, I decided to take days off to look for a non-war-industry job. I was interviewed at a lamp factory. Information about my having attended the University of Puerto Rico and having completed two courses in art with one in design appeared in my record.

I got the job! The lamp factory consisted of an assembly line, but this one was for painting eyelashes and eyebrows on the wooden animal bases of children's lamps. I painted lambs, elephants, and deer. It was boring, but the pressure was less than it had been in the radio factory.

One of the salesmen found out about my art and design courses, and he came to see me. He said that he would give me the opportunity to become a lamp designer because he was planning his own factory and wanted me to come with him and be his designer. I accepted his offer after he responded to my request to earn ten cents more an hour than my current job painting animals on lamp bases.

My workday in New York began by traveling underground at six o'clock in the morning on a train packed with people, nose to nose and buttock to buttock. At lunchtime, I would eat two pieces of bread with an inside "surprise" of cheese or meat that I had never eaten before, and milk or coffee that was so weak that one had to taste hard to recognize it as coffee. When the workday ended, I would head home to Alice's apartment on an underground train packed with others, like sardines in a can. I entered the train in the early morning and returned from underground only to find that daylight had already disappeared. The workday was difficult because of the constant efforts I made to understand the language of coworkers, people in the train stations, people at the coffee shops during lunchtime, and instructions from the foreman. Most of the time I understood what was being said, but the hard part came when I needed to answer. I tried as much as possible not to engage in full conversations, limiting answers to a simple yes or no.

These jobs in the factories during the first years of my life in New York City gave me direct experience with the problems that immigrants from Puerto Rico suffered. The difference with my experience was that I lived with a family that had been in New York for many years. Alice's father owned a *bodega* (grocery store). All of his children were protected and helped by him. Alice, his eldest daughter, lived in her own apartment with her three-year-old son while her husband was in the service. In the absence of her husband, Alice was well cared for by her father, even though she received all the benefits that a serviceman's family received.

In those days working in the factory, I sent almost everything that I earned to my family in Puerto Rico, keeping very little for myself. It was only when Belluci, my Italian friend, told me that I should open a bank account for my own needs that I kept some extra money for myself. When I think about it now, I realize that I did not even buy a life insurance policy from the many Metropolitan Life Insurance agents that used to come into our building every weekend. One agent was very angry when I grilled him about the benefits that I could get from the policy while I was still living. He asked me to leave when others copied me in asking questions about the benefits for those of us who needed the money for our day-to-day living.

When I look back on these first years in the city, I realize that the distance traveled from Puerto Rico in 1944 to New York City was not only in miles, but in time and years. It was like traveling from the nineteenth century to the twentieth century. The distance was also traveling from one culture to a completely different one. I had traveled the distance of language and culture. It was not simply the difference between Spanish and English, but the English of New York City in which "Jeet" meant "Did you eat?" I had never learned this type of English in my language classes.

The most taxing change in my life came from having to wear boots, sweaters, coats, gloves, a scarf, a hat, and earmuffs—clothing all made of wool. It was all so heavy and I felt so clumsy. This way of dressing increased my tiredness, because my small body had to carry so much weight. For many months, I lived as if I were in a dream. Fortunately, on weekends, Alice's father would come to take us out. Because he knew the city and we did not, he would invite us to special shows and outings. I remember with a warm feeling the first time I went to Radio City Music Hall. That Sunday afternoon will always stay with me as a beautiful and special experience of the city. The music of the show came out of an enormous organ like a heavenly serenade. The show was a program celebrating the music of George Gershwin. The ballet sent me into a trance. I had never seen such a thing. Following the dancers was a show that included live animals on stage, large waterfalls coming out of the walls, and a magician. But the most impressive part of all was the group of beautiful women dancing in perfect unison. I thought the Rockettes were magnificent! The rest of the show was a movie on the life of George Gershwin. As we traveled home that Sunday, my enchanted day ended with the music of "Rhapsody in Blue" resounding in my head. I had fallen in love with New York City in a love affair that would continue with a mixture of love and hate, as all serious love affairs often do.

I Become a New Yorker

What does it mean that I became a New Yorker? Was it the rejection of who I was at that moment in time? Or was this a positive state-ment of my having adapted to a new pattern for living my life? Now, as I reflect on the choice, it was not a rejection of myself or my country; it was an affirmative statement of the person that I wanted to become. Being a New Yorker meant that I had a broad new world of behaviors, associations, identities, and activities that I could enjoy. I would leave behind my poverty, my family pressures, and the constraints that I felt from the cultural and social expectations in Puerto Rico.

The first concrete change that I would make was in the area of employment. I was no longer a teacher. I was now a designer in a lampshade factory. This employment had exposed me to contact with a group of artists. When I began at the new factory as the designer, we were located on Seventeenth Street and Sixth Avenue. As the new business prospered and grew, the owners of the factory, William Zahn and his brother-in-law Jack, moved to new quarters on Twenty-fourth Street off Park Avenue.

Bill and Jack liked me very much and depended on me for new designs and production quality control. We had the kind of relation-ship that was sometimes strained. One of these instances was created when I discovered Bill had hired three new Puerto Rican workers, and they all had different salaries. I found out that all employees in the factory were Puerto Rican because Bill only published want ads in the Spanish-language newspaper *La Prensa*. None of the women spoke English well enough to carry a full conversation. Only one young man, a packer, spoke any English. I also found out that the women workers had requested a dressing room where they could change to their work clothing. They also wanted a couch in case anyone became sick during the day. I discovered that they knew nothing of workers' rights or the minimum wage requirement. Calling on some friends for information, I located a union organizer from the electrical workers' union and began to organize a workers' committee that would negoti-ate with Bill.

We found out about other violations and moved to open discus-sions with Bill for organizing a union and complying with workers' demands. When Bill learned that I had brought the organizer in the factory, he called me into the office and told me that I had betrayed him because he considered himself like a father to me. I reminded him that I could not have a blond, blue-eyed father, and that the workers were my people and he was exploiting them. After a long and heated discussion, he agreed that I would bring violations to him first and he would correct them. I agreed, if he remembered that I would speak to the workers first. We had many encounters like this one. For example, I had to request that he not interfere in my personal life when he "encouraged" a boyfriend, who would pick me up after work, to marry me. The boyfriend was José González, the merchant marine who lived in the house where I lived. Bill's interference caused José to have to tell me that he was married and separated from his wife. José then brought his child, and three of us started to go out together. He told me that his wife would not divorce him, so he could not ask to marry me.

Bill Zahn and I had a very good relationship as employer and employee. At one point, he told me that I needed an assistant because the workload had increased. I advertised for an artist in the art schools in our downtown area. Among the applicants was a student from Cooper Union who came to be interviewed. I selected her as the most capable applicant. Her name was Reba Joseph. She had come to New York City from Pittsburgh with three other artist friends. These women artists had obtained bachelor's degrees in art in a school in Pittsburgh, and had come to New York City to continue their art education at Cooper Union. They all shared an apartment in the Lower East Side of Manhattan.

Reba and I became friends, and she invited me to meet her roommates. My new friends, Betty, Gioconda Orestes, Helen Lehew, and Reba, shared a small apartment on 7th Street between Avenues C and D. The apartment's toilet was in the hall, and a tub was in the kitchen, covered by a metal slab that became their table. The other room was a very small bedroom. Seeing their space, I realized that my little room uptown was heaven. By this time, I had left the comfort of Alice's apartment and moved into my own furnished room.

The Years of a Bohemian Life

My new artist friends were interested in sharing expenses and finding a larger place. The night that I went for dinner to their place, we talked about a larger apartment, and I agreed to join in the plan. They secured four other female artists from Cooper Union, and the ten of us rented a very large apartment on the outskirts of Greenwich Village on Houston Street, next to the New School Workshop for Artists and the Jewish National Theater. This apartment was a delightful place on the fifth floor of a community house of an old church. In the main room of the church, where the benches and organs were still in place, a Korean businessman owned and operated auctions where he sold restaurant equipment. He rented us the fifth floor of the community house. He had already rented out the fourth floor that was an open space with showers to the New School Workshop for Artists. Many dancers and actors, who would later become famous, attended and practiced in the New School. Among them were Harry Bellafonte and dancers Marge and Gower Champion.

The apartment was perfect for our needs. It had a large kitchen with a black woodstove. From the kitchen, a hall led to rooms on each side. The bathroom, on the left side of the hall, had a wooden water box and chain to be used to pull the flush. The hall ended in a long room that was perfect for a studio. The studio had half of the stained-glass window depicting religious scenes. On each side of the hall, there was a total of five bedrooms. We could house two people in each bedroom. On the night that we found the apartment, I was invited by Helen to dinner to celebrate. That evening, we ate and then went to the roof of the house, where we sang songs from each of our cultures: "Hava Nagila" (Jewish), "Black is the Color of My True Love's Hair" and "Yankee Doodle" (United States), "Torna Asurriento" (Italy), and "Preciosa" (Puerto Rico). A week later, we moved in together.

Helen Lehew acted as my mentor, teaching me many things about musical compositions, composers of classical music, sculptors, and painters. I grew to love Beethoven, Richard Strauss, Mahler, Stravinsky, Prokofiev. We listened to these composers on the radio station WQXR. We visited the museums together to see the works of Van Gogh, Cézanne, Gaugin, Modigliani, Picasso, Diego Rivera, and Orozco. I agreed to pose for Helen. As she painted me, we would talk. Soon our apartment became a place where artists would come every weekend. If each of us invited five or more friends, we could easily have fifty people. Every person would bring something—a loaf of bread, a bottle of wine, cold cuts, cheese, fruits, éclairs, and other sweets. We had discussions on Frank Lloyd Wright and schools of architecture, Pablo Picasso's different periods of paintings, the Spanish Civil War and the Lincoln Brigade. We sang the songs of the war and we discussed Lenin, Trotsky, Stalin, Hitler, Mussolini, and Franco. We discussed the failure of Franklin D. Roosevelt to support the Jews and the role of England and France in the Second World War. We discussed the Bahai religion and other religions of the East. These were nights of great excitement and learning for me. We read poetry and selections of books in different languages. We read Kierkegaard, Jasper, and Sartre in English and French. I read to them in Spanish: Unamuno's "Cristo de Velásquez" and selections from García Lorca and Ortega y Gasset. Other people read Nietzsche and Rilke in German and Dostoyevsky and Tolstoy in Russian. I was learning and sharing in friendships in my new city. Our house became a school of art, politics, literature, and philosophy.

Our lifestyle was reckless. We drank a lot, and I am sure had drugs been accessible we would have taken drugs. We lived a life of experimentation and discovery. Ours was truly a bohemian life. I wrote poetry and fell in love with Lennie Maher. Lennie was a merchant marine and a lover of classical music. He had come to the apartment with one of the people who was a conscientious objector to the war. Alex, Lennie's friend, had been in prison at Levenworth, Kansas. One of the discussion groups that emerged was about the experiences of men who objected to the war for reasons of conscience. Both Alex and Lennie were pacifists. Both men had objected to the war. Lennie had joined the merchant fleet, but Alex had objected to the draft and elected to go to jail instead. Alex's parents were Hungarian Jews and Lennie's were Russian Jews. The discussions would move from the correctness of objectors to the war to the struggle of Jews to establish a homeland in Palestine. Alex had given up participating in anything and felt disaffected from the Jewish struggles. Lennie, on the other hand, explained that he was cooperating with the dream of a Jewish homeland by supporting the Hagannah. He gave me a book to read by

Arthur Koesler on the kibbutz in Israel.

We began dating, going to concerts, talking about literature during long walks together. On weekends, I would accompany him to his aunt's house in the Bronx, where we would pick up two suitcases. By the third trip, I asked Lennie, "What do we bring to your apartment from your aunt's home?" He explained that different members of his friends and family would bring guns, bullets, waterproof watches, and other objects that were needed by the guerrilla fighters. He would send them out to Palestine with friends who were merchant marines. I commented that if I were helping the fight for the homeland, perhaps his aunt would forgive the large cross hanging from my chain. Every time we went to his aunt's house, I hid my chain and cross inside my sweater. One night as we reached his apartment, he asked me to marry him. Sitting by the fireplace in his apartment while listening to Caesar Frank's concerto, I explained to him that I could not marry him. Lennie cried easily. That night he cried and told me that he would always remain near because I might change my mind someday. He knew Spanish and had written to my mother about his plans to ask me to marry him. I said that it would not be fair for him to wait around for something that might never happen.

Lennie did remain always near us, coming to the apartment after his trips. We helped him arrange for an Italian woman, Laura, whom he met by mail, to come to the United States to marry him. The marriage did not last long. She had used him to come to the States. We all loved Lennie as a brother. He returned to sail as a merchant marine and always sent us mail. Whenever he returned, we would go to concerts, the museums, and the ballet.

The original group of friends in the apartment remained stable, but others came and went. Most were struggling artists and students who held part-time jobs. They worked on special projects, such as preparing papier-mâché figures for the Christmas display windows of Lord and Taylor or painting portraits.

I remember that some nights, our dinner would consist of Spam cooked with cabbage and a glass of milk. We always, however, had money to go to the museums, concerts, and other art activities. Those of us who held full-time jobs shared with others. Betty and I paid fees for Gioconda, Reba, and Helen to become members of the Museum of Modern Art. A friend of Helen's, who played with the Pittsburgh Symphony, would give us special tickets for concerts. We were fans of the American Ballet Theater. I'll always remember the excitement of seeing the ballet "Pillar of Fire," with the music of the "Transfigured Nights" by Richard Strauss.

The Friday, Saturday, and Sunday night gatherings continued. Life in our bohemian apartment was disorderly and hectic. We all dressed in slacks and sweaters; our eating and sleeping habits were poor and disorderly. I would stay up all weekend. I could hardly go to work on Monday morning. Bill Zahn was getting very concerned about my lifestyle. One day he wrote to my mother about my way of life. His intrusion served the purpose of shaking me up and leading me to start thinking about my life and what I wanted to do.

Helen Lehew and I discussed our concerns, and both of us agreed that we had to move out of the church and set up an apartment of our own. Helen and I had been discussing the need to return to school. I had secured a better job as a youth worker at a community center. They needed me because I was bilingual. Helen's plans to return to school needed the confirmation of funds from her grandfather. We went on a trip to her family's home in Raleigh, North Carolina, and then on to her grandfather's house in St. Petersburg, Florida. She was in search of his commitment to pay her expenses to return to college. The trip was very successful. Helen's grandfather approved of the plan. He liked me very much, and we drove in his beautiful Cadillac from Florida back to Pittsburgh. The trip was a delight, even though the old man drove like a maniac.

I started my new job at the 110th Street Community Center in an agency started by a friend of Gioconda's. The new job called for me to dress in a different manner and required more traditional hours of work and play. Helen and I rented an apartment on the Lower East Side. She enrolled in NYU to finish a bachelor's degree, and I started to work regular hours. The job at the Center would reconnect me to my Puerto Rican roots, as it required that I interview Puerto Rican families to secure parental consent for their children's participation in the Center's program. My discussions with staff in this Center taught me many more things that were not necessarily part of the ideas in the Center.

In discussions with the work staff, I learned about the Jefferson School and began to realize that there was a gulf of separation between groups that had similar problems but never came together to work on mutual solutions. My interest in learning about different approaches to working with people and achieving understanding of their problems led me to continue my education. I attended a school at Sixth Avenue and 19th Street, where I took a class on "Marxist Interpretation of the History of Puerto Rico." I was the only Puerto Rican in the class. It was in this class that I learned for the first time that Puerto Rico had been invaded by the United States at the end of the Spanish American War, preventing Puerto Ricans from establishing their own revolutionary government. I learned that there had been a committee in New York City composed of Cubans and Puerto Ricans who worked and fundraised for the freeing of both islands from Spain. The section of this committee that had to do with Puerto Rico had made contacts with the president of the United States to insure that, if there were an invasion of Puerto Rico, the leaders of the committee would make up the new government of Puerto Rico. I had never heard this type of information spoken publicly nor had I seen it documented in print before. What I always knew was that we could only say that the United States had come to help our country. Only the revolutionaries of Puerto Rico ever challenged that idea. In this class, I also learned that Puerto Rico represented the naval door to the Caribbean Sea and to the protection of the Panama Canal. A document was made available to us that showed that there had been written communications between the Department of War of England and the Department of War of the United States, stating that England would maintain control of the Mediterranean Sea through controlling Gibraltar, and the United States would control the Caribbean Sea through Puerto Rico. The document stated that England was ready to support the United States in making that a reality. At the University of Puerto Rico and in high school, no classes in Puerto Rican history were ever taught.

This information was a great discovery for me, but it made me afraid. I was afraid of such ideas. I had grown up in Puerto Rico when it was illegal to fly the flag of Puerto Rico. I had witnessed the consequences of participating in demonstrations when a young man in my hometown had been shot. We had been raised in fear of any expressions or actions that could be used to accuse one of treason to the United States. I recall that when I first arrived in New York, I sent my mother a picture of me in my apartment with the flag of Puerto Rico covering the back of my wall. My mother wrote me immediately, chastising me for having the flag of Puerto Rico so visible in my apartment. She expressed her fear for what could happen to me and to my family back home. Today, such ideas seem silly, but it is important to remember that it is only in the most recent years that it has been legal to fly the Puerto Rican flag in Puerto Rico.

My new job at the 110th Street Community Center was an intriguing new experiment in bringing together white, Negro, Asian, and Puerto Rican families who lived and worked in East Harlem. The program did this by starting with a childcare service and addressing the problems of housing, health, voter apathy, and other common problems faced by these families. The Center itself had many internal programmatic and organizational problems, but my own development as a political person would soar forward here. The Center had a philosophy that the various ethnic groups living in the community should work together. This was a new way of thinking for me. I had never thought that these groups were disconnected and were not working together. This was my introduction to another type of racial conflict and prejudice. I had never heard or thought about these things in Puerto Rico. I learned that groups would not attend a meeting if too many Negro families attended. In addition to the racial conflict in the community hindering the Center's work, our daycare program did not succeed because there was dissension among our own staff. The executive director and his assistant did not agree to move into advocacy and militancy in finding solutions to the problems that the families were suffering. The program director, Alice Shiffman, and her husband held a radical perspective, were active in the labor movement, and held ideas about how to organize and move for action. They began to organize a union among the staff. The director, Mr. Culberston, who had been a minister, believed that people could hammer out differences and make decisions sitting around a table. As the struggle became an open fight, the union called a strike. The workers won the strike, and from that day on, the tension in the Center was disturbing to all of the workers.

I had developed a close relationship with Ruby Foster Shaw, a black woman, who also worked in the children's division. My other friend, Pat González, was a nurse. Both Pat and Ruby pressured me to return to school to finish my B.A. degree and prepare for a new job. I still had only a normal school certificate from the University in Puerto Rico. They informed me about the opportunity to complete college free at one of the city colleges. They were of the opinion that the Center would be closing because of its problems. Pat referred me to her friend at the Vocational Advisory Center, a free orientation service, where I would be tested for my vocational aptitudes and directed to return to school for a career. I followed this counseling, and Pat's friend became my mentor on my return to college.

While attending Hunter College, I returned to work part-time with Bill Zahn. My plan included enrolling in daytime classes after one semester of night attendance and securing a scholarship to supplement my part-time employment. The plan worked well.

To get to Hunter College, I rode the Lexington Avenue subway up and downtown, to and from my home on the Lower East Side, and to my part-time job at the factory on 22nd Street. I would buy a sandwich at an automat and eat it on the subway while I read my assignments. The financial situation was difficult, but we managed. I wore the same skirt and slacks all my years at Hunter. I used to say that if I put them on the subway, they would know where to go by themselves.

Third Part

A Builder of Institutions (1950–1960)

I Discover My Leadership Ability

When I entered Hunter College to complete my baccalaureate degree, I began to seek new social and personal connections that would replace the loss of my community of artist friends. During those years, Hunter College provided little in the way of experiences with other Puerto Ricans. I joined the European Club, but, unlike the people that I had met in the artists' circles, these students were, in my opinion, elitists and insensitive to issues of race and gender. I can remember a very strong argument with a German Jewish girl who considered herself an intellectual. She insisted that women had made "no contribution to the advances of the human race." I became so furious by such a ridiculous statement and many others that I finally left the group. I was feeling isolated and without any social connections. Helen and I continued to have friends for dinner, but a void existed for me.

At school one day, I met Maggie Miranda who was in my sociology class. This was a class that I enjoyed in which I would argue with the professor and challenge many of his statements. I connected with Maggie because she was a Puerto Rican. We became friends, and through Maggie I was introduced to the Spanish Club. Here again, I found myself out of place and with people with whom I had little in common. Maggie knew other Puerto Rican students, and I suggested that we meet with them. One by one, we met each other in my apartment. When the group became too big, we secured a room at the Good Neighbor Community Center on 106th Street in East Harlem.

These were the years from 1950 to 1953, when I was finding my way to a New York Puerto Rican community. My activities now included community events and meetings with a group of young people, most of whom had been born in the city. I was a part of them, but there were differences. I had lived previously in a different environment from most of them. I was almost five years older. I lived in my own apartment. I had emigrated from my own country, leaving my family behind. I had the experiences of living in an early bohemian commune environment.

I often thought that I was now friends with young people who had lived near me in the Bronx and had mocked me by calling me "Marine Tiger" (the derogatory name for Puerto Rican immigrants who came to the United States by ship). I was to discover a new set of friends and began associations with Puerto Ricans who spoke English better than Spanish, and who had never been to Puerto Rico, although they had strong feelings of attachment to the country. I was forming the associations and friendships that I needed. Although we had these differences, we built a strong bond that would become the foundation for forming strong new institutions and sustaining lifelong friendships.

During this period, the daily newspapers were carrying many articles about the problems that Puerto Ricans were bringing to the city. All the reports were negative. We used the group discussions to share our feelings of isolation and dislike about the representation of our people. At first, we were only students, but later nonstudents were added to our group. The first members of the group were Maggie, Miranda, Marta Valle, and Sandra Canino. These were the Hunter College students. The nonstudents were Joe Morales, Annie Class, Charlie Cuevas, and Paul Caballero, who were employed by the Office of the Commonwealth of Puerto Rico. This office was a branch of the Department of Labor of the Commonwealth of Puerto Rico, which played a strong role in the life of Puerto Rican New Yorkers. After informal meetings and discussions, we decided to formalize our meetings and recruit other young people who were not affiliated with any other groups. Our discussions covered many issues: Why did our parents emigrate? Why do Americans hate us? Why do Americans accuse our women of being prostitutes and our men of being lazy?

Why are we accused of coming to New York to get on welfare? Why? Why? Why? We had long heated discussions for hours into the night. We were discussing and educating ourselves. We began to formulate our own ideas about what was happening to our people. We came to the conclusion that our parents and relatives had emigrated from Puerto Rico, meeting many problems that they did not know how to solve, because they did not know the language and did not understand how the government functioned. We also examined the existing Puerto Rican organizations and concluded that they also did not know how to solve the problems. Above all, we concluded that we were not the problem. These problems were here before we had come. These were the problems of New York City.

Although the Office of Puerto Rico had been established to assist in problems of employment, social welfare, migrant workers, housing, and general transition, we believed that it should also train leaders and new community organizations and groups to work with the people. We began to formulate our own philosophy for helping our community. We believed that organizations should be developed to handle particular types of problems and that they should concentrate on developmental approaches that would educate to prevent future problems. We described this approach as one of community development instead of "firefighting." We also believed that the organizations should be held accountable to the community, governed and managed by Puerto Ricans, and that the city government should be held accountable for offering services to our community.

Our meetings became social and learning sessions. I did not believe that we should continue meeting without taking action. We named a study committee to propose how the group could become an instrument of work. As a result of the committee's recommendations, we developed bylaws for an organization, and we voted to become advocates and policy monitors of government agencies and elected leaders. We also voted to take on action projects. These recommendations would actually result in the creation of a formal organization with bylaws and officers. I was elected president by acclamation. We called ourselves the Hispanic Young Adult Association (HYAA). This name would later be changed to Puerto Rican Association for Community Affairs (PRACA) after the organization had increased in strength and visibility.

HYAA became very active and well-known in our community. Our first action project was with a local church in East Harlem. We cleaned, painted, and furnished La Misión de Rescate in the basement of a building that the church used as a shelter for homeless men. A minister of a small church, who lived in an apartment in the same building, sustained La Misión with donations from his salary as a factory worker. We secured monies in donations from businesses, churches, and community leaders. In addition to the painting and plastering work that we completed, we secured beds and linens, dishes and clothing for the men. We prepared a budget and taught the minister how to administer the donations.

Our second project was to establish a voter registration office and head up a drive in East Harlem. After studying the list of registered voters, we selected an area with a heavy concentration of Puerto Ricans. We organized our members in pairs. They were assigned to go to the Puerto Rican families and provide them with transportation and accompany them to registration and voting locales. We visited the candidate for City Council, Robert Low, whom we supported after examining his qualifications and interviewing him. We requested that he pay for an office, provide us with materials for working, and requested his commitment that if he were elected, he would give attention to the problems of our community.

As time went on, we worked briefly in a housing clinic of the Office of Puerto Rico, but we left this project because it was absorbing too much of our time and energy. We settled upon an idea to organize a Puerto Rican high school youth conference. We said that this would be a youth conference where the youth would present their problems. We wanted the young people to talk to us and to talk to each other, thereby breaking the traditional format of adults talking to youths or about the youths. Youth would talk for themselves. We organized ourselves into committees to work with the young people on the different aspects of implementing the conference. Certain guidelines were set: All speakers would be youths; adult participation would be limited to the audience; young people from high schools would be members of the planning committee and all other working groups; an evaluation would be conducted to assist the youths in continuing conferences in the future.

The first Puerto Rican Youth Conference was so successful that eight subsequent high school Puerto Rican Youth Conferences were held. These conferences forwarded the basic idea for developing a youth movement service agency.

HYAA had integrated our social and personal lives. The youth conference influenced us profoundly and secured a sense of responsibility and purpose for us. At the moment when we were experiencing and working on these activities, there was no other group like HYAA. We were not a funded agency with staff. We were volunteers. All our work was done by the members of HYAA. We were highly organized, keeping records of our work, holding planning sessions to initiate new activities, and conducting yearly evaluation meetings in a summer camp that we organized. We were a new and unique organization in the Puerto Rican community.

As the group grew and became more sure of itself, I raised the issue of the group's name and why we called ourselves Hispanic and not Puerto Rican. Most of the major groups serving Spanish-speaking populations were all called Hispanic. I expressed my belief that we should call ourselves Puerto Rican, and I asked all Puerto Ricans to raise their hands. The only two members who were not Puerto Rican were a Jew and a black who were friends of members. I asked, "Are we ashamed of calling ourselves Puerto Ricans? I think that we should change our name to identify our Puerto Rican origin." I opened the session to discussion. Joe Morales, the member from the Office of Puerto Rico, was the leader of the members who did not want to change the name. The discussion became bitter and would be the first of many heated discussions. Finally, someone suggested that we identify other possible names, including HYAA, and called for a vote. PRACA received the majority of votes. We changed our name that night.

I cannot begin to state the strong impact that this group had on all of us. There are members of the group who remain friends or are married to other members. Others still keep contact with one another. The marriages included Luis and Cecilia Núñez, Joe and Josie Morales, Max Gonzales and Annie Class, and Marta Valle and Charlie Cuevas. Eddie Gonzáles, Alice Cardona, Yolanda Sánchez, Maggie Miranda, and Josephine Nieves have remained good friends throughout the years. Other good friends are Bernie Roseman, Carlos Dominici, Paul Caballero, Mary Balladares, and Sandra Canino.

We had one annual event that promoted fraternity. Every summer the group would go to the camp in Harriman State Park to evaluate the work of the year. By this time, I worked for the Union Settlement House and had the use of their camp. We sang the songs of Puerto Rico, told stories of our families, played games, danced, walked, and developed a strong sense of solidarity. Our social activities were accompanied by discussion groups and presentations. We evaluated the work of the group during the previous year and planned for the coming year. We discussed the history of Puerto Rico, our culture, the problems of our community, the lack of education for our children, and injustice and discrimination in the society. We also discussed program ideas and made assignments to committees that would plan and conduct upcoming projects.

Although Joe Monserrat, the head of the Commonwealth Office, assisted in the early stages of our work by allowing us to meet at his offices and by arranging exposure and educational trips to Puerto Rico, I was aware that we had different philosophies of organizing and working with people. I had immigrated to this country with the knowledge of its long history of oppression and injustice against our people. The government of the island had no announced policy with regard to the emigration of our people to the United States. The Commonwealth office said that it neither encouraged nor discouraged emigration, but provided services once we had arrived in the city. The leadership of the office espoused integration and assimilation, but I knew that only those of us who were white-skinned had any hope of this kind of acceptance. Our group was not promulgating assimilation into the life of the city as an explicit philosophy. It was clear to me that I was the leader of the group, and I felt that I had the responsibility of continuously bringing these issues to the group's attention. I expressed my thoughts in the group discussions. However, the issue of race was never directly handled.

I have always believed that my ideas were in conflict with those set forth by the Office of the Commonwealth of Puerto Rico. The people in our group who worked at the Office believed that their mission was to help the community solve its problems. Others and I believed that the Office was equally concerned with maintaining a position of control over New York Puerto Ricans and keeping the leadership in the hands of the government of Puerto Rico. The differences of opinion continued to be a part of the life of our group. Now, many years later, there are documents that indicate that our emigration was an essential part of Operation Bootstrap, the government policy that advocated the displacement of Puerto Ricans from the island as a way of supporting the efforts of planned economic growth. Documented evidence also supports my idea that the Office of the Commonwealth did indeed have a policy of assimilation and control over the growing influential community of Puerto Ricans on the continent.

As the activities of PRACA took on more visibility and challenges, my life at home and with my Puerto Rican friends was becoming more separated. I was very conscious that I now had a private life and a public life. As the New Yorker that I had become, I learned to separate them. I created my own public life. Public affairs, socials, parties, and dances began to be part of my work. These were opportunities for people to consult with me. I was being seen as a person of leadership and wisdom. I tried very hard to disappear from crowds after I spoke or after the ceremony had begun. I have always been and continue to be uncomfortable in social settings. In the beginning, when I learned that people would seek my opinions and be influenced by my advice, I felt afraid, and I reflected on many occasions in my early life when I had taken the position of influencing childhood friends or family members. I began to consider very seriously the new leadership role. There were no role models for me, and I knew of no classes where I could learn. I decided that this was a very important ability that I had, and I had to be careful and responsible in its use. I developed practical guidelines for working with people, which included the development of skills, sharing leadership, accountability, and self and work evaluation. I used these principles for future institutions and efforts that I would undertake with others. This public-private separation that I had elected to take would continue throughout my life. I allowed very few people to share close connections with me.

A Graduate Student

Becoming a social worker was not my first choice of professions. I had come to the United States "to study medicine" as a way of securing permission to leave Puerto Rico during the war. I had been a teacher in Puerto Rico, obtaining a two-year normal school diploma, the most a poor person could aspire to. The diploma was the fastest road to getting a job teaching. Ultimately, my choices of profession were made by what was possible for a person who did not have the means to acquire more education. When it came to social work, I knew that I did not want to be a caseworker, since I believed caseworkers participated in making people adjust to situations that they should fight against, situations that hurt them or rendered them powerless.

After two years of study, I graduated from Hunter College and was admitted to the Columbia University School of Social Work (known at that time as the New York School of Social Work). During my last year at Hunter, through a library search, I had identified a scholarship called the Antoinette Cannon Foundation Scholarship. This foundation was headed by a social worker who volunteered at the Office of the Commonwealth of Puerto Rico. I requested an interview with her after I had submitted my application. The Commonwealth Office where Ms. Cannon volunteered was headed by a person who knew me from Puerto Rico when I was very young and had spent time in the Aibonito Preventorium recovering from TB. Her name was Ms. Matilde Pérez de Silva, and she gave a glowing recommendation of my work in the community. I was awarded the fellowship and entered my first year of studies.

My life in the New York School of Social Work was full of many challenges and struggles. My choice was to enter the community organization program with the intention of pursuing social policy and administration. Making the decision was easy, but getting it approved became a big problem. I had to see my faculty advisor for his approval. He met with me several times to convince me that this was not a good choice for me. He proposed and would approve of my selecting the group work program. After my pushing hard, my advisor informed me that "over his dead body" I would enter community organization. He elaborated by saying that it was his responsibility to "guide" me into the choice that he felt would offer me the best opportunity to obtain a job upon graduation. This "guidance" interview ended by my signing up for group work after his extreme pressure, but I decided to choose all the courses that could be used as possible electives from the community organization concentration. I graduated with a heavy number of courses in community organization, but with a concentration in group work.

At this point in my life, I did not fully understand such advising as racist or the use of "guidance" interviews to track minority students. My advisor did not expect that I, a Puerto Rican woman, would have any opportunities for positions in administration, fundraising, or advocacy that were the employment goals of students entering the community organization concentration. It was much later on my road to becoming a full New Yorker that I understood the pieces of that dialogue that had not been verbalized. However, my experiences in the school would help me to understand the relationship of power between myself and my advisor, a white male.

I completed my first year using my savings and my fellowship. Helen and I had developed a plan to pay expenses as we both continued school, but the second year was approaching. The registrar told me that the school would like to know very early if I would enroll for a second year so that it did not use resources on a person who could not return to graduate. She, dispassionately, adviced me to withdraw from school, go to work, save money, and return when I had funds for tuition and expenses for the second year of school. She asked me to think about her suggestions and to return when I had an answer to her proposal. I left the interview in a fury! My anger at the woman was so great because she and my advisor were standing at the "gate" to prevent poor persons and minorities from entering. There was no effort on her part to offer avenues of securing economic assistance. This was my first encounter with the exclusionary practices that kept poor minority students out of prestigious graduate schools. Several days after discussing this incident with Helen, we decided that I would return to school and make clear to the registrar that I was returning and I would have the funds for my second year. In a different tone, the registrar informed me that she was concerned about my facing a problem later on.

After this experience, I began diligently to search for fellowships and financial aid. I found a fellowship called the Opportunity Fellowship awarded by the John Hay Whitney Foundation. I applied and, after several interviews before the end of the first year, I received the announcement that I would receive the amount to cover the second year's tuition. I would be able to cover my expenses by taking positions at a nursery on East 27th Street, and during the summer I would work as the director of a special project in Bridgeport, Connecticut, studying the conditions of poverty of Puerto Ricans living in Bridgeport. It also required that I organize an association of residents that would remain as a liaison to communicate with the mayor. The project was paid for by the office of the mayor and conducted through Hull House Settlement. The executive director, Mr. Ewell Newman, was very helpful in my success with the study and the organizing aspect.

My courses at the School of Social Work helped me in designing the study, preparing the questionnaire, training the residents to function as a research team, and organizing a group of street captains who would obtain information on the residents in the neighborhoods. The captains called weekly meetings and kept records of the problems that residents had. Through the study, we located a number of families who rented apartments in basements, where parts of the floors were made of wood. Others had no floor and the bare earth was visible. The apartments had broken windowpanes covered by the families with cardboard. Back doors were broken, allowing cold winds to enter the apartments. Cold winds and generally poor living conditions kept the children and adults sick. Many of these families had applied for apartments in public housing projects that had been constructed and remained empty, but the families' applications had been rejected. I started a series of phone calls to the Housing Authority inquiring as to why the families had been rejected. I also began inquiries to find out the extent of vacancies in the new development.

My research informed me that there were many empty apartments in the two housing projects and that there was an unsolved struggle between city and federal authorities that had resulted in not renting a very large number of the available apartments. However, I was not able to convince anyone that my families needed housing before another winter. I returned and informed the association that my efforts were in vain. After a long period of angry comments that expressed their powerlessness, I proposed a course of action, which contained elements of risk for all of us, including me. I would go to the settlement house that sponsored the project to ask for the military tents they used in summer camps for children. The tents would be raised in the city park, and the families that had been denied housing would come with their clothing, their pots and pans, children, and other belongings, and sleep there until the authorities would come to find out why we had moved there. They agreed, and I asked the director of the settlement house for the tents. He agreed to lend them. The men in the group, under the direction of a staff member of the settlement house, set up the tents in the park. No one came to ask anything, so we brought the families. I stayed to sleep with them. Very early in the morning, police on horseback came to awaken us. Newsmen from the city's two newspapers and officials from the city came to ask who had given permission for us to move there. I explained the situation, identifying myself as the director of the Mayor's Project on Puerto Ricans in Bridgeport. There was a lot of back and forth between the police and the city officials. I said that there was a very easy solution in that the public housing project had empty apartments and my families had applied for them. After the newspapers took photographs and copious notes on our description of the group and how we arrived at the decision to sleep in the park, the police told us we could not stay in the park. I asked if they knew where the families could go. The city officials had already called the mayor, and the Housing Authority staff came in to take the names of those families that had applied for housing (which were all the families I had selected to move into the tents). Before the end of the day, families were assigned to apartments in the housing projects.

I was called to a meeting with the mayor at the settlement house. I was asked to communicate with the mayor's office before taking such drastic measures to solve problems. I explained that I had tried to speak to someone with authority to act. I asked why families that lived in basements with wooden floors and broken windows and back doors could not occupy the empty apartment units, but the housing official explained that there was an impasse between the mayor and the federal authorities that held up all decisions on renting these apartments. I ended my presentation by saying that a ridiculous situation called for a drastic action on the part of the community, and so we took action. From then on, the mayor appointed a small committee that would meet with me weekly to handle any problems I needed assistance with. I used the incident in a written assignment in one of my classes in the School of Social Work the next semester!

There are decisions you make that affect your life and the lives of many people around you. I learned and relearned this many times in my life. At the job in Bridgeport, I learned this in a very real and dramatic way. The lives of those families were changed, but also the Association of Puerto Ricans in Bridgeport remained after I left, as an instrument for them to continue to work with their problems, and with the help of two powerful institutions: the settlement house and the Catholic dioceses, which continued to work with the network of captains I had started. However, I reconfirmed my conclusion that in order to create change, one would have to know how to affect the policy formulation processes in the society. My hard work in Bridgeport did not change the basic policies of creating and assigning housing to families who needed it. I know that those who pass laws, and assign public funds to create housing, do not provide in the law for the housing to reach those who need it most. I also learned in that project that even if the housing is provided by formulating policies for it, those who implement the policies could violate the intent of the policy. I reconfirmed and increased my desire to study the field of social and public policy and how these provide for, interfere with, or deny resources to provide people with healthy and productive lives.

Working at the Commission on Intergroup Relations

The years 1957 and 1958 were of momentous importance to my work as a community developer. I was thirty-one years old and had completed my professional education. I was continuing my work in the Puerto Rican community as my major personal and professional concerns. I had not yet discovered what institution-building was, it was during these years that I took my first steps down the road to becoming a builder of institutions. Although I do not remember who asked me, or under what circumstances, someone asked if I was a social worker. My immediate and automatic answer was, "No, I am a builder of institutions." This answer made me ask myself, "What is a social worker? Isn't that the profession that you studied?" I had a very interesting dialogue with myself. I said, "Yes, I did attend a School of Social Work and graduated with a master's degree in social work." Throughout all my years of work, I continued in this ideological separation from the profession, causing me eventually to abandon any affiliation with it. Social work education had the objective of separating me from my community and making me a "professional." I had to find the way to become an agent of change, working in partnership with the community of which I was a member. I had learned in my relationship with my community that we could work collectively to find solutions to our problems. As a member of the group that had left the island, I knew that we possessed the courage and stamina to leave everything behind and start anew in an unknown land. I knew that we could build new lives in the city while preserving our culture in our institution-building to create our community life. I did not want to see myself in any profession that implied or indicated a separation from my community.

Very soon after I graduated from the Columbia School of Social Work and began work in the Union Settlement House, I stopped being a social worker in the traditional sense of the work. I left the job at the Union Settlement House when a position was offered to me to become a member of a small group of people who would work on a new city commission. The person to head the commission was Dr. Frank Horne. My name was presented to Dr. Horne by the executive director of the John Hay Whitney Foundation. Both were black men who belonged to The Forum. Dr. Horne would later explain to me that The Forum existed in the South to advocate collectively for important policy-making structures in the national government against racism. It is important to state these details because I had never fully understood the term racism until I went to work for Dr. Horne. The small staff under his leadership was to create a city agency from an executive order of the mayor.

Participating with Dr. Horne in building the commission was a great learning experience in how to build an institution. I was able to see how the political factions of the city had to be manipulated by using the power of the political party in office, which at the time was the Democratic Party under Mayor Robert Wagner. We had to use the commission to make an institution that would act to create change for the minority populations who were excluded and oppressed. Our activities had to be undertaken in such a way that we could bring about change without threatening the powerful real-estate lobby, banking industries, and other powerful interest groups. The key to the success of the commission's work was to be able to create a city agency that could accomplish two objectives: (1) to bring about change for those who suffered discrimination and exclusion; and (2) to educate the larger society by using the expressed values and public policy of a democratic society.

Our work was conducted through intensive meetings held every day, lasting all day with one break for lunch. When I returned home in the evenings, I was exhausted but exhilarated by the realization that I was participating in a history-making activity with people who were teaching me a great deal. Each day we engaged in discussions, under Dr. Horne's direction, about the philosophy and the structure of the problems to be addressed and the programs to be offered. I learned about the history of racism against blacks, Jews, and Native Americans. I learned in detail of national studies concerning discrimination in housing and employment. I learned of the historical struggles taken in the courts to affect the problems of exclusion. I learned about the National Association for the Advancement of Colored People (NAACP), the Urban League, the American Jewish Committee, the American Jewish Congress, the Anti-Defamation League, and about the struggles of organized labor, the exclusion of Catholics, and the efforts to establish coalitions among the excluded groups. Above all, I learned about the history of blatant and open destruction of black people in the United States, where the lynching of black men was not punished by the legal institutions of the states. These were facts that I had never known. I was finally able to understand my experiences of coming to the United States through New Orleans. Even though it may sound incredible, it was in those planning meetings that I fully realized and understood that I was a black woman and that in Puerto Rico, being black was a lesser condition than being white, that although racism was not practiced in the same manner as in the United States, it was nonetheless practiced effectively.

I came to understand that the creation of the commission was a political maneuver that had to be understood and used with great finesse, because of the delicate balance of political power among groups in the city. Our struggle had to be fought not only within intergroup relations in each locality, but also in the courts of the nation through the legal processes. The most important lesson that I learned was that each group that was oppressed and excluded had to learn the nature of its particular situation, establish lines of cooperation with other communities in the struggle, and organize institutions to fight against the insidious and destructive process of racism and exclusion. My experiences in working in the Commission on Intergroup Relations helped me to see Puerto Rico and its relationship to the United States in a very clear light. I began to read avidly about the history of the arrival of U.S. troops on the island of Puerto Rico.

In developing the commission, Dr. Horne and the six original staff members established communications with the oppressed communities of the city. To fulfill the requirements of the executive order, departments were organized that responded to issues and problems that created destructive intergroup tensions. These were identified as housing, the schools, employment, and police relations with poor, excluded communities. The most important problems were identified as discrimination in housing and the integration of children in public schools. Meetings were scheduled with the main leadership of the ethnic and religious community organizations. The mayor was given advice by the ethnic and religious leaders in naming commissioners who would be the policymakers. This was a highly political activity. Dr. Horne maneuvered himself through these sessions with great ease.

I saw the processes of the political relations of a city like New York in action. I witnessed the strength of the labor unions, the influence of the religious organizations, and the relative weakness of the racial and ethnic groups. I saw the complete weakness of the Puerto Rican community. No Puerto Rican commissioner was elected.

The importance of having selected me to be a member of this staff was very clear to me. I realized that I had to use this opportunity to the maximum. The group of six original staff members selected by Dr. Horne were: Corinne Morrow, an expert in housing, well connected in Washington, D.C., and longtime friend of Dr. Horne; Mr. Sidney Frigand, a public relations expert with strong relations to the newspapers and strongly connected with the leaders of the Jewish community; Paul Klein, a longtime friend of Dr. Horne from the Jewish community and longtime friend and worker with Mr. Thurgood Marshall and the legal department of the NAACP; Cyril Tyson, a very bright young man, well connected to the Harlem leadership and, at the same time, to the newly emerging leadership of the Muslims; Harold Hunton, a young man well connected to the hierarchy of the Catholic community and its church. I was the sixth member of the original commission staff.

We developed a very close relationship to Dr. Horne and one another. Before new staff was added, Dr. Horne stated to the six of us that if we had a special project we needed to work on that had an important meaning to our community, we should bring it to his attention and we could use the commission to make it a reality. I immediately thought of the project I had written and brought to the Union Settlement House and to Joe Monserrat. I asked to see Dr. Horne and presented the idea verbally. I summed up the idea as an effort to develop new young leaders in the Puerto Rican community of the city. He told me of his experience in having organized in the South a group of young black professionals who called themselves The Forum, with the purpose of identifying problems and ways of dealing with them. He explained that a lot of the work he had done in housing was the result of the work of this group. After a very amenable conversation, he asked me to have the project written up and typed and to give him a copy. I went home that night, flying high with joy, and asked Helen to review my grammar on the document. The next day, I brought in the project to be typed by my secretary, asking her to place a copy on Dr. Horne's desk. The name of the project was "New Leaders in New York." I still have a copy of it. Dr. Horne called me to a meeting two days later and gave me extensive verbal and written advice as to how to proceed with the project. He said he would give me other feedback as he thought further on it, but asked me to proceed to work on it using the commission resources.

That night, I went home very excited. I called all my friends who had worked with me in PRACA and its youth conferences. I felt that a milestone had been reached, and that I was on my way to doing something very important. Cyril Tyson also presented a project to work with the young leadership of the Muslims in Harlem. Periodically, we would speak to each other about our progress in working on our special projects. In the commission, we were working on inter-group relations, as required by the mayor's executive order, but most important, we were organizing a knowledgeable new leadership in parts of our communities that had never received the opportunity to work for our people. This was a purpose never intended by those who created this commission.

The New York City Commission on Intergroup Relations was officially organized with several departments: a strong department that received and investigated complaints on discrimination in hous-ing, headed by Corinne Morrow; a department that worked with the Board of Education and the major black community institutions on the integration of the schools, headed by Cyril Tyson; and an inter-group relations and tension control department, headed by me. Each department hired other staff members, and we settled down to work, offering reports to the commission at its monthly meetings. Neither Tyson nor I reported on our "special projects." I knew that my special project would be the way to begin to bring Puerto Ricans into action in New York City and to help obtain a degree of power. Dr. Horne was offering me a way of strengthening the Puerto Rican community so it could work on the solutions to its own problems and have a voice and a presence in the city. I made up my mind to use the opportunity that he had opened. Very soon Dr. Horne called me to his office and intro-duced me over the telephone to a friend of his who was the executive director of the New York Foundation, Mr. Sol Markoff. Dr. Horne left us speaking after suggesting that we arrange to meet on the project that I was trying to create. Markoff was key to the rest of the fund-raising efforts for my project and was also a source of advice on the development of the institution we created. He was instrumental in securing the initial grants from five foundations to start the project.

At this point in my life, I realized that the choice I had made to turn down a Fulbright Scholarship to study in Europe after graduating from Columbia and accept the job with the Commission on Intergroup Relations marked the beginning of a very crucial epoch. It was as if a very wise and powerful voice inside me was saying, "You wanted to learn about policy, how it works to deprive people of their rights and how it can also be an instrument to empower people to secure those rights. Well, here is a real-life situation to learn, and you do not have to go to school outside the country to learn it."

Fourth Part

The Puerto Rican Forum (1957–1964)

I had received advice from Dr. Horne and Mr. Sol Markoff that it was urgent that we move "the project" for the Puerto Rican community out of the commission. Horne explained that if the project was organized on the commission's time and with the commission's resources, it belonged to the city of New York. He urged that the project should be born as a Puerto Rican initiative. He advised me to organize a board of directors that would take the leadership. Markoff agreed completely and further added that the board should be made up of Puerto Ricans. It was much later that I fully understood the significance of this, when we were challenged from the outside, and even within our own group, to integrate the board.

I organized the group that had been working with me to develop a youth program into an organization called the Puerto Rican-Hispanic Leadership Forum. In our discussions, we aspired to developing more than one institution, because the Puerto Rican community in New York did not have its own institutions. Other ethnic and racial communities had organized themselves to offer services and to fight for the rights of their people, such as the Urban League, the NAACP, the American Jewish Committee, and the Anti-Defamation League. We foresaw that the Puerto Rican Forum could become the founder of needed Puerto Rican institutions. The name "Forum" came out of the story that Dr. Horne had told me of the group to which he belonged. The word "leadership" was included because we all thought that we needed to develop a group of committed leaders who would engage in the work needed to service our problems and fight for our rights. The word "Hispanic" crept into the name because in those days (as is true today), there was the notion that we needed to include other Spanish-speaking groups in our activities in order to obtain strength. The words "leadership" and "Hispanic" were dropped from the name later, when the Forum became more certain of itself.

The first effort to organize a board of directors came very early, as were our meetings to secure funds and adopt a name for the entity. The organizing group was made up of some of the original people from PRACA and others who became interested in the idea. We had our first disagreement around our fundraising efforts. Two or three members suggested that it would help the fundraising effort and bring us more prestige if we appointed a non-Puerto Rican to our board. The name of the young man who was the son of the chairperson of a leading foundation in New York was proposed. I opposed the idea on the grounds that if we opened the door to one foundation, we would have to open membership to other funding sources. I also argued that we had enough prestige in our own reputations and positions. We decided that prestige, self-respect, and recognition had to come from the work that we accomplished and not from people outside our organization. The idea that we were the source of our own prestige was an idea that the group accepted, and we remained confident through all the projects that we would create. In all of our future projects, the issue of an all-Puerto Rican board or an integrated board would come back many times. We would also be accused of separating ourselves, although we were following the pattern of other ethnic and racial groups.

In establishing and incorporating the Puerto Rican Forum, we had a dual purpose. First, because we believed that the Puerto Rican community did not have solid information about the nature and scope of the problems that it faced, we decided to become the source of that information and serve as the "forum" to interpret it. Second, we were going to establish institutions headed by an intelligent, knowledgeable, and committed leadership.

The Forum was organized as an instrument for us, as Puerto Ricans, to create institutions that would fight to eliminate the problems that were making our community weak, poor, silenced, submissive, and convinced that they were the cause of their own poverty and exclusion. We gathered information, conducted studies, held forums and discussions on each of the problems that affected us, and created an institution that would deal with those problems. The group immediately agreed to become the first board of directors of ASPIRA, the project that the Commission on Intergroup Relations wished to transfer to them. A committee of the board was set up to name and establish the new entity. The Forum made the decision to spend its time and resources on making the new organization an instrument to develop leaders from among our youth, who were becoming dropouts and losing their identity and connection to their community. The committee gave the project the name of ASPIRA, the command form of the verb in Spanish meaning "to aspire." The group selected Frank Bonilla, a young Puerto Rican sociologist who was working at a foundation, to be the first president of the Forum.

Originally, the Puerto Rican Forum was conceived as a "launching pad" from which satellite institutions would be created to work on their individual areas of responsibility. This was a beautiful idea, but when the time came to put the idea into operation, the Forum had problems letting its offspring go. Once its first organization, ASPIRA, had become an accomplished and well-recognized entity and even owned its own building, some members of the Forum board did not want to let ASPIRA go. It took many heated discussions regarding the philosophy and mission of the Forum before a final vote approved the original decision and steps were taken to incorporate a separate board and obtain tax-exempt status for ASPIRA through the pro bono help of lawyer Harris Present, who would help out with all our institutions. The building we had acquired had been registered as the property of ASPIRA.

The discussions and the actual act of liberating ASPIRA led to the reaffirmation of the Forum's philosophy and our commitments to each other. It established a new way of working together. We had learned how to disagree without becoming enemies and to retain respect and trust among ourselves. Most important of all, we developed a sense of community that very few Puerto Rican groups in New York had achieved. I know that without the kind of trust and friendship that we established during those early years, we could not have attained the degree of development that the Puerto Rican Forum reached. I still have loving warmth for my colleagues many years later, and we remain friends. I realize today that I matured into full adulthood during those years. In the middle of activity that influenced the lives of many people, I did not realize that my work would be of such future historical importance to my community and to the city. It was only when I became the executive director of ASPIRA that I began to realize that our work would change the lives of many Puerto Rican youths and their families. As I write this book today, I continue to learn about the full impact of the work that we have had.

With the experience that the Forum gained in creating its first institution, the board began an examination of new problems that it could address. At the same time, a new public policy was announced by the federal government to designate funds for assisting the poor in establishing instruments for their own empowerment. Our board felt that we had the experience, knowledge, and philosophical understanding to work on a project that could address the community's poverty. We were an institution that had worked before anyone ever mentioned the War on Poverty. We had worked, placing our time, intelligence, energy, and personal funds together, to develop the organization. We had tested experience. We felt called upon to establish a citywide effort to assist all the existing Puerto Rican organizations in our community to develop the best War on Poverty effort in the city of New York. This commitment led the Forum to embark on its second project, the Puerto Rican Community Development Project in 1964.

ASPIRA, the Most Important Work of My Life

If you asked me, "What was the most important and impacting work that you have ever done?" I would reply, "The founding of ASPIRA." ASPIRA occupies a very special place in my heart. Trying to tell the story will be very difficult. Don Miguel de Unamuno, the Spanish philosopher and novelist, once said that a sheet of paper is dead and incapable of transmitting the emotions one wishes to convey. My words are clumsy in English and may be unable to capture the feelings that I wish to transmit. I will try, however.

The idea for a youth project began out of the early work of

PRACA and its youth conferences. The conceptualizing of the ideas continued throughout my education as a social worker and during my association with Puerto Rican youths while working at the Union Settlement House. The ideas lived in my mind and on pieces of paper, but the full implementation did not come about until Dr. Horne supported the effort through the Commission on Intergroup Relations. This time period actually spans over seven years, ending in 1961. As I reflect on it now, I had begun to consider many theories of group work and development when I was a student at the New York School of Social Work, but I had not begun to think of program ideas. When I graduated from the School of Social Work, I went out of my way to find a job in the Puerto Rican community commonly called "El Barrio" in East Harlem. I could not be employed in a Puerto Rican agency, since they were non existent. I opted for the best substitute in selecting the Settlement House on 104th Street between Third and Second Avenues. I was employed as the director of the adult program. There were only two Puerto Ricans on the staff. Although situated in the heart of El Barrio, the Settlement House did not attract many Puerto Ricans because they did not speak English.

While working at the Settlement, I continued to share an apartment with Helen, but we had moved to a small unit in a renovated apartment building on 97th Street, between Lexington and Third Avenues. While we lived there, I found myself relating more and more to the Puerto Rican community. Helen would accompany me to some of the activities, but most of the time I would attend alone. Our lives began to go in separate directions. After a big disagreement, we separated our lives, and I continued to live in the apartment until I applied to buy a cooperative apartment at La Salle and 125th Street. The meetings of PRACA could now be held comfortably in my new apartment, since it was big and beautiful. My house became the center of activity for the younger professionals in the Puerto Rican community. I began to be considered the center of the group.

The original idea that I presented to Dr. Horne was called "New Leaders in New York." It was to organize youths into clubs that would become the vehicles to encourage them to find their identity, learn leadership skills by working on problems that their communities suffered, complete high school, and enter college to pursue a career that would allow them to give back to their community. The idea had germinated in my mind as a result of various experiences that I had when I arrived in New York. The idea began to haunt my thoughts after having heard discussions from Puerto Rican high school students who attended the youth conferences that PRACA was holding. These conferences were organized and held by the youths themselves, who were the leaders and speakers telling us how powerless and insignificant they were made to feel by their classmates and teachers. The students discussed their fear of speaking in their classes, their shame because of their native language, their fear of the gangs from other ethnic groups, and their fear of the police. I was deeply concerned about what I was hearing.

The implementation of my ideas would not come easily. I had to pursue many different persons and approaches before I could succeed. At the Settlement House and through the activities of PRACA, I had become more deeply committed to a program of action that would change the lives of these young people. As I would walk to my job in El Barrio, I would see a group of Puerto Rican teenagers standing in front of the settlement, engaging in what seemed to me a strange ritual: taking turns spitting. I would say, "Good afternoon." There would be no answer. One early evening as I prepared to visit the adult club meeting, I noticed a young man leaning against the wall in front of the door to my office. He seemed to be a member of the group that I had seen spitting in front of the building. I said hello and he responded. I seized the opportunity to ask if he was a member of the youth program on the fourth floor. He replied no, but said that he had come to speak with me if I had the time. When I said that I had the time, he sat down and opened with a barrage of questions, one right after the other.

What was my position in the Settlement House? Since I had an accent, was I a Puerto Rican? Did I go to school in New York?

I answered the questions as he asked them. Then I asked one question, "What is the game that I see you and your friends playing outside? The spitting?"

"It's a contest. Whoever spits the farthest, wins."

"Wins what?" I asked.

"Wins nothing."

We continued to talk about the fact that he lived in the Bronx, but came to East Harlem to visit his friends. He worked in a shoe factory downtown. His name was Eddie González, and he was seventeen years old. He was one of fourteen children. He had dropped out of school to help support his family. The González family was on welfare, but he had to supplement their income, since sixteen members needed his help. Eddie confessed that he was sorry that he had dropped out of school, but he considered it too late to return. I shared my experiences of going to night school and using vocational services to plan to complete college. I encouraged him to consider that he was young enough to return to school to complete his high school education at night and still continue to help his family. He argued that he was too old to return to school. I shared my experiences of attending night school with many adults who were his age or older.

I invited Eddie to join the group called HYAA. Later on, Eddie did complete his education and left his own impact on the city of New York by helping a whole generation of Puerto Ricans to obtain leadership positions in the labor unions. He developed a union leadership institute at Cornell University.

The experience with Eddie propelled me into writing the project for leaders of the new immigrants in the city. My idea was to pick up youth and provide a way for their "hanging out together" (the clubs), following a behavior that was natural to their age group. In the clubs, they would learn about their culture and the country of their parents, and also learn how to survive in the school and the neighborhood. The club would provide opportunities to develop feelings of self-worth and appreciation for their culture as they learned leadership skills to work in their communities. The clubs would substitute for the gangs that were already becoming popular protective groups for Italian, Polish, and black youths.

I worked on my idea of developing youth clubs by researching how the Jewish community had developed its youth programs. I also studied the literature on youth gangs and their origins. This information was becoming available through the city's newly organized agency, the Youth Board, an agency that had been formed to work with the existing gangs. I studied the literature to understand what components had made movements such as the Catholic Church survive and endure over centuries of time.

Youth gangs had become a serious problem for the city. Gangs organized themselves along a racial or ethnic identity. Puerto Rican gangs had already emerged to provide answers to problems that the total society had created for Puerto Rican youth. In the gang, they found the power, prestige, economic means, and a community of identity through organizing and establishing such symbols as jackets and names that meant power and elicited fear. I thought of the club as a means to provide every one of these needs. I played with symbols and ceremonies that would relate to our political situation of belonging to a nation that was captured by and permanently occupied by the United States. I researched how the youth institutions of the Catholic Church and the Jewish community appealed to their members, and how they had survived through centuries, even facing opposition and persecution. The document I was writing changed over many revisions.

First, I approached the Union Settlement House to try to institute the project, since it had no program for a community that lived at its own doorstep. Bill Kirk, the director of the Union Settlement, suggested that I should present it to the association of Settlement Houses. I approached an officer of the association, and he answered that it could not be done by them. After putting it away for a while, I presented it to Joe Monserrat, the director of the Office of the Commonwealth of Puerto Rico in New York City. I tried to interest Joe in the idea, but he would not sit still long enough to listen to me. A member of HYAA, Joe's secretary Annie Class, asked me if she could type the document, and place it on Joe's desk, so he could read it in peace and quiet when he read his mail. I thought this was a good idea and asked her to go ahead. He never touched the document. It sat in the same place we had placed it for two weeks. I decided to go in and pick it up from his desk and take it home.

Meditating about it, I thought maybe the idea I proposed was not urgent enough in the constellation of grave problems Joe had to deal with. In his position in the Office of the Department of Labor of the Commonwealth of Puerto Rico, he had to attend to the scope, nature, and size of problems that accosted our community in the city of New York, but he also had to provide services and solutions to the problems of contract workers who came from Puerto Rico to work on farms, picking vegetables from the eastern seaboard to states in the Midwest. They came for help to the offices in New York, with problems ranging from physical abuse to dealing with poor food, inhumane dwelling places, and abusive treatment from the foremen and the owners, as well as violations of contracts regarding pay. Joe also had to deal with problems brought by immigrants to the city such as unemployment, inhumane living conditions in apartments in the slums of the city, police brutality, ill treatment by the public school of parents and students, tensions in the neighborhoods, indifference in the social services departments and others.

Despite these being immediately urgent situations, I thought we had to get out of the "firefighting" position that we were in. We needed to design ways to attack the root causes of these myriad fires and begin to develop in the community other people who would join the battle at different points in the problems. The approach I prepared suggested two roads: the immediate help brought by youth clubs that could engage in giving attention to selected problems; and the longer road that would develop educated leaders committed to the resolution of the problems at policy levels, in the political and economic spheres of the total society. I concluded that either Joe had no vision for the growth of our community in the city, because he had to respond to the wishes of the political leadership in Puerto Rico, or he was threatened by the potential creation of a group of young, educated, and dedicated Puerto Rican New Yorkers who could challenge his position as sole, top leader and spokesman for us, representing us to the overall city leadership. At any rate, I concluded that ASPIRA became a threat to him.

When Dr. Horne agreed to listen to my ideas and support me, I was delighted and excited. I began calling a number of my friends to tell them that we finally had support. Copies of the original papers were passed around to a group of five of my friends who were working with me in PRACA.

After months of work, our group had prepared a philosophy, a mission, objectives, and a work plan. Everyone agreed that this new leadership program should not become a service agency; instead, in form and methods, it should be a movement. However, we all were wise enough to understand that it had to render some service if it was to be successful in raising funds.

The very important act of naming the project engaged the group in discussions that clearly indicated a philosophical position and a profound understanding that to work with youth we had to impart values, optimism, and the decision to succeed. We wanted an upbeat name, one word to express belief in one's self. The word *aspira* was finally selected. It was chosen because to aspire is upbeat. We all wished the meaning would be "I will aspire and I will attain." The Spanish command form ASPIRA, of the verb *aspirar,* was perfect.

We made fast progress in organizing ASPIRA. Dr. Horne's introduction to Mr. Sol Markoff, executive director of the New York Foundation, went a long way toward making our proposal more fundable. Horne introduced me to four other foundations. A couple of board members and I met with representatives of these foundations to present and defend the proposal. We were all novices in such matters, but we were able to obtain interviews with five funding sources: the New York, the Field, the Hofheimer, the Rockefeller Brothers, and the Taconic Foundations. Sol Markoff became our mentor and our facilitator during these interviews. All five foundations approved requests for funding. In fact, after a few months of functioning, we approached the Taconic Foundation. They suggested that I increase the amount requested, and funded us for three consecutive years, pending the positive evaluation of each year's work.

In the autumn of 1961, we received letters from the five foundations accepting our proposals and assigning funds. The Forum board called a meeting to discuss what to do, since we now had funds to start the project, but no one had ever had the experience of administering an institution. At the meeting, they all concluded that I should resign my position with the city of New York to come and direct ASPIRA. I postponed an answer until I had spoken with Dr. Horne. He agreed with the board: I should leave the Commission and become the first executive director of ASPIRA. He acknowledged that it was risky to leave the security of city employment, but he said that I was the only person who could get ASPIRA going. It must be understood that I had never directed an institution, but with the help of all my friends, I took the job. And I learned on the job as problems emerged and needed to be resolved.

The physical work and good social times were accompanied by long and arduous hours of discussion and decisions. We wanted to develop a program that would work with youths in groups because we believed that that way, it would be economically feasible to reach large numbers of young people. I had been a group worker, and I also knew that the adolescents would be most influential on each other. We planned for the groups or clubs to be organized in schools, in churches, on street corners, in billiard parlors, or wherever young people congregated. The youths would be asked to organize their own ASPIRA clubs, and by following a list of eight required steps, they would be accepted into a federation of clubs. Once the groups completed the eighth step, they would be initiated through a ceremony called *areyto*. The idea of the *areyto* had been borrowed from a ceremony of the native Taínos (the original inhabitants of the island of Puerto Rico who used the ceremony to celebrate their leaders).

From the beginning, ASPIRA adopted three major objectives in working with youth:

1. To organize a youth movement in the Puerto Rican community that would learn leadership skills, problem identification, and problem-solving skills, and to work through the clubs and the club federation in resolving the problems of the Puerto Rican community of New York.
2. To help club members study the history and the culture of Puerto Rico, as well as the history of their parents' immigration to New York, and to use this knowledge to develop a commitment to and positive identification with their community, in order to strengthen their participation in the life of their community.
3. To stay in high school, to graduate, and to identify a field, profession, or area of work in which the youths could earn a livelihood and acquire the skills to work as a leader in the communi-

ty. The federation bylaws spelled out the number of youths allowed in each club, the naming of the club, the community projects to be selected for the club's work, the selection of career study areas, the assignment of a staff person, and the training and responsibilities of personnel to work with youth.

Our planning went very well. However, immediately upon opening our doors for service, a series of internal problems with the board and members of the community emerged. The members of our board had never served before on the board of directors of an institution. The Puerto Rican community of New York had never had an institution that offered services with a staff and formal offices. So, neither the board nor the community knew how to relate to their new institution.

An example of the kind of problem that I had to resolve with my own board came very early in the life of ASPIRA. At one of the early board meetings, the chairperson requested monies to establish a bar for the meetings. I would not approve the expenditures of grant funds for purchasing rum, beer, gin, ice, cheese, crackers, lemons, or mixers. I added that the idea was a good one, however, and I placed $20 as my donation to support the idea of the bar. I requested that board members do the same. I further requested that a proposition be introduced for a vote that would establish the policy that funds donated to ASPIRA could not be spent on activities or items for the benefit of the board, because it violated our tax-exempt status. A long and heated discussion followed with the board finally approving a policy that established the board's respect for donated funds and our responsibility to use funds only for the objectives of the specific donation.

The board chair was seriously opposed to the decision, above all objecting to the right of the executive director to oppose the board and its desires. He called for an executive session that would exclude the executive director from discussing this issue with other members of the Puerto Rican Forum. The original decision was ratified, and it was further stipulated that the executive director had the right and responsibility to raise questions about the expenditure of funds or violations concerning the mission and philosophy of the institution. This was a very good issue to come to discussion in the early life of an organization. Even though I felt good about the end result of this first struggle, I was upset because it resulted in a tense relationship between the chair of the board and myself.

Problems that we encountered as we began to be known in the community were created by our community's lack of knowledge and experience in relating to an institution and in the feelings of some community members that felt they had a privileged status because they knew members of the board. For example, members of the community who considered themselves "important" would bring or send their children to request scholarships without belonging to or working in the clubs. In other instances, board members would send relatives or friends to obtain jobs for which they had no skills or for jobs that did not exist. The examples were numerous, but they always reflected a desire to obtain special privileges or resources. These problems and complaints were discussed at our board meetings, and were at times used by others to say that ASPIRA was not serving the community. I held firm in refusing to compromise our funding obligations and our mission and philosophy. As ASPIRA became better known, these problems diminished.

The most serious and destructive problems came from other youth and educational agencies and from non-Puerto Ricans. Very serious examples of these were hate letters, tapes, and recordings sent to me personally and to ASPIRA. Threats of violence were received whenever there was a news article announcing our receipt of a grant. I opened a file on these letters, following the advice of the police. Other less violent attacks came from people in the audiences at conferences where I was invited to speak. Members of the audience would angrily ask why we were segregating our youths into separate clubs and why we Puerto Ricans needed help in adjusting to the city when other newcomers had to make it on their own. Other youth-serving agencies attacked the idea of our setting up a separate new agency instead of bringing the funds and our youths into already existing programs. Fortunately, no physical attacks were ever made, only threats. From these experiences, I learned how to handle myself and to deflect the attacks. Sometimes I would respond directly and harshly. Other times, I thought it best to throw the questions back to those who challenged our work.

By far, the most difficult opposition came from the Board of Education, which wrote to ASPIRA saying our counselors would not be allowed to counsel the students because they were not licensed. I wrote back stating that we did not want the licensed counselors of the Board of Education to counsel our children because their advice was destructive to our youths' future. In the end, this was a function of ASPIRA that the board could not control, since our educational planning and counseling was conducted in the clubs at ASPIRA's offices. Later on when we had many clubs, they met at schools, but by then ASPIRA had enough strength to overcome the Board of Education's protests.

One of the really destructive acts of the Board of Education was not to allow the organizing of ASPIRA clubs in schools with high enrollments of Puerto Rican students unless a teacher was present at all times. This was fought vehemently by ASPIRA at the Board of Education level because it involved the attendance of teachers in meetings after school hours, for which they were not compensated. ASPIRA collected information on other student organizations, such as Hillel, NAACP, Catholic and Protestant clubs, and other ethnic youth clubs, such as the Irish, Spanish, and Italian clubs. ASPIRA was able to win recognition for its clubs, but the issue of the presence of a teacher advisor to be present at all meetings remained. The youths were able to convince some teachers to fulfill this requirement.

The club programs grew to be very impressive in membership size, number, and impact. The ASPIRA Club Federation became a very powerful organization with very successful programs. The most notable ones were the summer leadership study trips to Puerto Rico, the annual conference to evaluate and plan the federation program, the *Areyto* Leadership Initiation Ceremony, the Annual Graduation Dance, and the Annual Colleges and Universities Fair. The important fact about the model of the work in clubs was that it was invented by the youth.

About two weeks after we opened the offices on West 72nd Street in Manhattan, a young woman came in and asked if she could meet with the director. I received her and she proceeded to tell me, "I am a high school student in Brooklyn. I read in the newspaper that ASPIRA is organizing Puerto Rican youths in high schools. I came to inform you that I already have organized my own club in our high school. We met and decided that I should come to find out how you will work with us. We are ready."

I was very impressed with this young woman's aggressive approach. I asked for her name and how she had organized her club.

She said, "My name is Migdalia Torres de Jesús. I simply called together a number of my friends, and we each brought a friend. Those interested in continuing to meet and find out how the new program could help us were asked to sign a list, leaving their name, address, and telephone number. I spoke to them and read them news about ASPIRA offering help with graduating, going to college, and forming a club to study our culture. I said, 'Don't sign up if you are not interested in this.' Mostly, all those present signed. Then I was selected to come and investigate what you will do for us."

I said I would assign an organizer-counselor to set up a meeting of the club to find out what individual help each member needed and to inform them about other requirements for initiation as an ASPIRA club.

Migdalia asked for a specific date when her club would come to Manhattan to meet in ASPIRA's office. We designated a date, and she left, but not before asking if I would give permission for the club to announce that they were the first ASPIRA club. I said they could, and we said good-bye. Migdalia was a real find. She taught us how a club had to be organized by the youth.

This was not the only time that staff of ASPIRA learned from Aspirantes (the youth members of ASPIRA) how to organize the movement that was ASPIRA. On another occasion, during the beginning of our institution, we struggled with the idea of creating a federation. We already had clubs in the Bronx, Manhattan, Brooklyn, and in the central office, which we called "home clubs." These clubs consisted of youths that either were not in school or were so few in their high school that they could not organize a club. Our conference room was always full of young people. One day a group of young people requested a meeting with the staff and me. They said they had a proposal to present to us. At the meeting with us, they stated, "We think that in order to make a reality of the idea that Aspirantes have the strength to be a force in the fight for the rights of Puerto Rican students and adults, the clubs should be organized into a federation of clubs called the ASPIRA Club Federation (ACF). On the blackboard, they drew a scheme showing the relationship of each club to the federation and the relationship of the ACF to the ASPIRA board of directors. It was a delight to see the youths already becoming a force for change, seeing themselves as joining the strength of loose clubs to a body that could influence the board of ASPIRA. I presented their scheme to the board of directors, since it included the proposal that the ACF elect three members to the board of directors of ASPIRA! The proposal was accepted, and today in New York and in the ASPIRAs in other states, the ACF elects five members to the board of directors of the agency. The ACF in New York also proposed to the staff of ASPIRA that an association of parents of club members be organized.

The expectation was that the ASPIRA Club Federation could be an instrument of power for the Aspirantes, to be exercised against the power of the overall society when it used its strength to oppress the youth. This principle was tested in a demonstration staged in front of Governor Nelson Rockefeller's house. The ACF was protesting the City University of New York raising its admission requirements. The governor had approved these "higher" standards. The CUNY tuition-free colleges were the institutions that most of the college-bound Puerto Rican high school graduates attended. Most Aspirantes planning to attend CUNY held jobs after school while in high school in order to contribute to their families' income and in order to buy clothing and books for themselves. The announcement of the higher required grade point so late in the school year gave them no opportunity to raise borderline averages. The ACF and the parents' association mounted a picket of a three-ring line consisting of a man, a woman, and a student, symbolizing a mother, a father, and their child. The picket was led by parents holding a casket they borrowed from one of the Puerto Rican funeral parlors. On the casket, they placed a very large sign that said, "Rockefeller, you killed the future of high school Puerto Rican youth who worked all year to attend CUNY and now cannot make it." The picket line circled the block where Governor Rockefeller had his New York City home. The press and television covered the orderly picketing, chanting, and marching. The mounted police were there the whole time to keep order. We, the ASPIRA staff, were deployed at key spots across the street from the picketing to prevent provocateurs from causing trouble. A student and a parent were spokespersons to the press and television. Leaflets explaining the situation were distributed. It was a successful demonstration. The governor's office asked ASPIRA, the ACF, and the parents' association to meet and give them a list of the affected students. All students affected entered college the next autumn.

The reader will understand why ASPIRA became the most important work of my life. In terms of numbers, ASPIRA of New York alone, from 1963 to 1999, can easily be shown to have touched the lives of approximately 36,000 young people from Puerto Rican and other Latino groups. This is a conservative estimate, using the number of thirty clubs a year with twenty members each—and we know some years we had many more clubs, and some were larger. But numbers do not tell the complete story. So I must tell you about the principles, the values, the philosophy upon which we, the founders, built the model of service. The most important of these has been the grounding of ASPIRA in the knowledge and value that people are born, grow up, and develop fully and best in a community. We believe that the uprooting of our children from their community has been deadly to their ability to learn and to their sense of worth. The immigrant family did not have the supportive environment of an extended family, neighborhood, and friends. Human beings live in families and in communities because they need these for their survival and development of their full potential. I challenge this society to test these statements and to find out if these are the reasons why our youths have so many problems in the United States.

A second principle upon which ASPIRA was founded is that there is a continuous developmental chain that prompts the emergence and maintains the growth of leadership from one generation to another. In order to provide a community with those leaders, it needs to identify and solve its problems and to guide the group through good and difficult times. That leadership emerges in a continuum through the contact and education of potential leaders from one generation to another. The potential leaders must have the opportunity to challenge and take over the mantle of leadership from older, established leaders.

Potential leaders must engage in the educational process that affords them the opportunity to learn history, new technology, and skills that will help them to identify problems and learn how to solve them. Leaders, new and old, must engage in the development, nurturing, and demonstration of ethical commitment to their communities.

Another important pillar in the founding of ASPIRA was the need to establish an institution that would insure that the youth of our community would be educated to acquire the knowledge and skills available to grow fully to their maximum potential. We also hoped to insure that they could occupy positions at all levels of the institutions of the society and earn a living, but also contribute to the needs of their family, their community, and the total society.

The challenge we imposed on ourselves was to invent a model that would operate on those principles, values, and philosophical commitments. We succeeded in doing so. Today, there are Aspirantes who went through the process and are in leadership and professional positions throughout the city of New York and in many other cities across the country. They work in corporations; in city, state, and federal agencies as top leaders; in universities; in social and educational agencies at top-level positions as scientists, entrepreneurs, and artists. Some have returned to serve as staff or board members of ASPIRA in various states. They make real the commitment that they pledged while they were members of a club. Many of the Aspirantes are engaging in organizing new agencies to deal with community problems. Others have played central roles in organizing ASPIRAs in other states. Today, there are seven ASPIRAs: in Connecticut, New York, Pennsylvania, Illinois, Florida, and Puerto Rico. They are served by a national office in Washington, D.C.

I left ASPIRA of New York in 1966. For several weeks, I drove across the United States to see the rest of the country. The real and most important reason for my trip was to disconnect myself from the organization. I wanted very much for the board to select a new director without any input from me. I had been in the position since 1961, and I felt that it was time to leave. I was the only director that the board and staff had ever known. We had learned together and grown together as a family. I was leaving the agency to take a teaching position at the Columbia School of Social Work, my alma mater. I was leaving the agency in the hands of Yolanda Sánchez, the program director who had been my student, while a new director was being selected. Louis Núñez was the assistant director of the institution. In these two persons, I believed that there was significant experience and sense of continuity to move forward. I also had decided to leave because my philosophy of leadership has always been that the top person must step down to open up opportunities for new people. In spite of my convictions that I was making the right decision for myself and the agency, I felt sad because I was leaving friends and an organization that had become a big part of my life, and its people had become family to me.

Since leaving ASPIRA, I have been fortunate to have visited all of the affiliates and to attend conferences, participate in the inauguration of new centers and in graduations at their schools. I am most satisfied and feel a great sense of pride to know that the work that we began in 1961 continues and has made an impact on the lives of thousands of young people.

Whenever I travel to give speeches, receive awards, or attend conferences, I always meet Aspirantes who share their accomplishments with me and thank me for having made the resources of the institution available. I have heard their wonderful stories as I travel from one end of the country to the other. I hear these stories from faculty, elected officials, businessmen, artists, scientists, writers. Without a doubt, I feel enormously proud as I refer to all these people as "the children that I had."

When I hear of the problems of any affiliate, it pains me in a very personal way. Over the years, I have heard negative comments and criticism of ASPIRA. From time to time, I am told that individuals have used an affiliation with ASPIRA to advance their own careers. With regard to those who have claimed a relationship to the founding of the institution, I can only say that many persons supported our efforts, including Puerto Rican teachers, community leaders, and aspiring political figures. I wish to acknowledge the support of the community in our work. For those who have used positions on the board or staff for personal advancement, I have nothing to say.

Criticism is difficult to accept. ASPIRA has been accused of "creaming," by serving students who are already bound for college while not maintaining sufficient activities to reach and motivate the truly needy. I know that, over time, the ASPIRAs may have yielded to the obligations of funding sources and reshaped their original objectives. I have always directly criticized the pattern of fundraising that obligates an institution to one major source of funding or to a governmental funding base that too frequently controls and alters the original mission of an institution. Also, I have always been clear that it is vital to maintain the base of ASPIRA as a Puerto Rican entity, although other populations are served.

Over the years, I have been asked to meet with ASPIRA students. While I lived in Puerto Rico, they would visit me yearly as part of their annual trips. I have always been asked questions regarding the origins, mission, and objectives of the institution and the relevance of maintaining an institution that is Puerto Rican. I have not always felt that my insistence on maintaining certain founding principles has been well received by new boards, but I have been consistent in my position that ASPIRA is not simply a service entity. It is supposed to be a movement with a national network that acts as an advocate for youths and their community. The ASPIRA bilingual education consent decree, won at court, was one of the major efforts that grew out of this tradition. Many Young Lords Party members and leaders in "the student revolts" developed or reinforced their sense of cultural identity and affiliation as members of ASPIRA clubs. Members of the first graduating clubs of ASPIRA entered college and formed the pivotal base of movements for Puerto Rican Studies programs at universities.

The charge that ASPIRA was founded as a conservative social service entity is simply not true. I challenge any critic to review the original documents to determine the true nature of our intent and our commitment to social change.

The Second Institution: The Puerto Rican Community Development Project and the Study on the Poverty Conditions of Our Group

When I reflect on the beginnings of the group called the "Young Turks," I cannot help but be impressed by our accomplishments. I feel proud of the part that I played. If our intention was to change the attitude of Puerto Rican New Yorkers about what they could do and who they were, I believe we succeeded. We demonstrated to ourselves that once we identified ourselves as a community, as Puerto Ricans, we could build our own institutions, fight our battles, and become New Yorkers. When I arrived in the city, there were no Puerto Rican institutions. The existing groups in which Puerto Ricans were participants were called "Hispanic" and "Spanish American," despite many of them having a majority of Puerto Rican members.

There was a Spanish judge who was considered by the city political and bureaucratic leadership as the spokesperson for Puerto Ricans. His name was Emilio Núñez, and he belonged to an organization formed by Spaniards in the city. Since no one challenged him, Judge Núñez spoke for Puerto Ricans before city agencies and the press. Later on, the Office of the Commonwealth of Puerto Rico Department of Labor took on this role, again unchallenged. As a result of the institution-building work of the Puerto Rican Forum, many organizations began to call themselves "Puerto Rican." We in the Puerto Rican Forum and in ASPIRA were able to establish a healthy identity and vision of our country of origin and the home of our parents. After the romantic dream of returning one day to live on the idealized island was dismissed by many of us, we grew up without rejecting or condemning Puerto Rico. We saw Puerto Rico as it is. We did not hide or deny our critical assessment. We, Puerto Rican New Yorkers, Nuyoricans, made the decision that our lives were going to be lived in New York, and we had to find a space in it, no matter how difficult the city was. We concluded that we had to find that space, hold it, and fight for our rights and acquire the strength, knowledge, and courage to succeed in that struggle. I have participated in many of the battles of that struggle.

As I mentioned previously, the Puerto Rican Forum was our instrument to create other groups and other institutions, other service programs, and other instruments for developing a community that had no voice and no access to its own empowerment. The first step in this direction was to give leadership to ASPIRA, the first funded and professional staff institution of Puerto Ricans in New York City. The second concrete step was to create a citywide institution to fight poverty by establishing a community development institution with funds from the federal War on Poverty program.

In 1960, President John F. Kennedy launched a program called the President's Committee Against Juvenile Delinquency. The agency provided funds for communities to create their own approaches to rescuing their youths from engaging in juvenile crime in gangs. One of the better known programs funded by these monies was called Mobilization for Youth on the Lower East Side of Manhattan. A member of our group, Manny Díaz, worked in Mobilization for Youth, and through him, we at the Puerto Rican Forum knew of the approach taken by the program in their fight against juvenile delinquency. The basic philosophy was that the community had to organize itself to rescue the youths from forming gangs. I agreed with this foundation for a program against delinquency, but I disagreed with Mobilization for Youth's concept of community. It considered the "community" as the geographic neighborhood in which the youths lived. We in the Puerto Rican Forum knew that our community could rescue our adolescents if "community" was understood to be the group with its culture, its language, its patterns of behavior in the family. Because Puerto Ricans lived throughout the city, it was not possible to fight for our youths with these monies, because there was no distinct geographic area that was Puerto Rican. Furthermore, we had no citywide organization in our community that could apply for the funds and organize the program.

In meetings of the Puerto Rican Forum, we had discussions about the need for a citywide council of Puerto Rican organizations. Many of us, individually and as members of PRACA, had participated in work of the Council of Spanish American Organizations that had been organized by the Office of the Commonwealth of Puerto Rico. We had withdrawn from the council because it did not have the strength, the skills, or, above all, the independence from the government agency to be able to develop and administer programs to fight juvenile delinquency among our adolescents, or any other program to fight for our rights. We, the social workers in the group, were very critical of the fact that the council could have served as our entity to fight for our rights or to conduct activities on our behalf, but it was too dependent on the government agency of Puerto Rico to be an effective representative of our communities.

Following the assassination of President Kennedy, Lyndon B. Johnson entered the White House and launched a comprehensive program to help poor people. Not only was he interested in working with the problems of delinquency and youth gangs, but he expanded the War on Poverty to include the idea of "maximum feasible participation of the poor." This expanded direction had the stated goals of teaching and empowering poor people to engage in the planning and implementation processes that would bring services, resources, employment, and housing to their communities. The idea of having the poor act for themselves was a key concept in any request for federal funds to address poverty.

I remember that the black community moved to create a structure that could use the funds by developing a major comprehensive effort to mobilize poverty-stricken families out of the chronic conditions caused by poverty. The project was called Harlem Youth Opportunities Unlimited–Associated Community Teams (HARYOU–ACT), which was organized primarily to serve Harlem. The leadership organizing the project invited me to be a member of its board, and in the course of attending the planning meetings, I gathered information and began to understand how a similar organization of Puerto Ricans could be created to secure the funds offered by the War on Poverty. The only group in our community that had the skills and intellectual resources to undertake such an effort was the Puerto Rican Forum. I brought the information that I had acquired to the Forum, and it agreed to research how we could educate a group of our leaders and organizations throughout the city about the existence of these funds and how Puerto Ricans could create an organization to secure money to fight the poverty of our people.

After discussing the fact that we were the poorest group in the city and how the Office of the Commonwealth of Puerto Rico in New York City acted to retard our development, a decision was made to proceed with the development of an effort similar to HARYOU-ACT. I was very vocal in bringing to the discussion something that had never been spoken about, although many leaders had feelings about it. I spoke about the fact that the New York office of the Department of Labor of Puerto Rico offered very important services to the newcomers arriving from Puerto Rico, but it also played a paternalistic role toward those of us who had been in the city over an extended time and who understood exclusion and discrimination. We wanted to act to change the situation. I presented my opinion that the Commonwealth of Puerto Rico had become an appeaser and compromiser by providing seminars and workshops for police, teachers, and welfare workers. These were the city officials and the professionals who would not serve us. These were the same people who denied us our rights. I spoke of the well-known trips to Puerto Rico provided by the Commonwealth offices to heads of agencies and political leaders and city officials to the island to discuss us and the problems that we brought to the city. I stated directly and clearly that this was the only role they had taken. The discussions culminated in our decision to undertake a different approach, exercising leadership based on the facts of our condition. Although there were members who opposed my position on the Commonwealth, in the end the board of directors of the Puerto Rican Forum requested that ASPIRA grant me a leave of absence so that I could become the director of the six-month poverty program if we were able to secure the funds. With this decision began the resentment and anger that would ultimately destroy the Forum's vision for the project to fight poverty among Puerto Ricans. One of the members of the board was against my being selected as the director of the project. He became one of the leaders of the opposition throughout the life of the pilot project.

I agreed to head the project because I thought I could do a good job in achieving the expected products and goals in the limited time available. The expected goals were to conduct a study of the poverty conditions of the Puerto Rican community of New York City; design a program that would attempt to change the poverty conditions identified by the research; form an incorporated, tax-exempt organization with a board of directors, which would solicit funds within the requirements of the War on Poverty; and establish a pilot program in the South Bronx.

In six months, I initiated an educational process of Saturday seminars attended by leaders in the Puerto Rican community. The seminars focused on the legislation, philosophy, and methods for eliminating poverty, and studied the existing projects. Staff from the Washington office of the War on Poverty, heads of foundations, city officials, staff from HARYOU-ACT, university professors, and community leaders from the Lower East Side project were seminar presenters. The participants used half the day to discuss and begin to envision possible approaches our community could use to fight the ravages of its own poverty. This process culminated in the organization of a board of directors and the formation of an organization that they named the Puerto Rican Community Development Project (PRCDP). A planning grant was requested and approved by the city agency working with Mobilization for Youth. The grant was awarded to the Puerto Rican Forum to hire staff to achieve the goals listed.

In keeping within the guidelines of the War on Poverty of "maximum feasible participation and grass-roots community involvement," the PRCDP had created a plan that was comprehensive in design and provided for the development of the existing agencies, and grass-roots organizations within the New York Puerto Rican community. Many years later, we would learn of some of the inherent contradictions and problems related to translating philosophical language into practical applications. Our plan envisioned a mechanism for community-building with overarching goals, permitting the various participant-groups to come together to implement the plan with their resources and areas of skill. The plan advocated a model of comprehensive community development and advocacy, as opposed to a fragmented and disjointed service delivery network. Seventy-eight groups endorsed the plan. The actual project directors and members at large totaled sixty-nine persons. The executive committee included Dr. Francisco Trilla, Joseph Erazo, María Canino, Rev. Pablo Cotto, Monserrate Flores, Gerena Valentín, Father Walter Janer, Julio Hernández, Luis Quero Chiesa, Max Sanoguet, and me.

As stated in the document, the plan set forth six basic principles:

(1) services would be offered to all who requested them, regardless of race, religion, or national origin; (2) its board and policymakers had to be Puerto Ricans; (3) the board of directors would guide, administer, and evaluate the programs and organizations funded by the project, but it could not use its power or staff to control or weaken them; (4) programs or organizations funded had to have their own boards to administer funds for the programs, hire staff, decide questions of policy, and, in general, play their proper role as independent boards; (5) whenever possible, indigenous personnel or "sub-professionals" would be employed in the neighborhood orientation centers and organizations receiving aid and they would receive proper training and function under the direction of competent staff; (6) the PRCDP would be an instrument to help Puerto Rican New Yorkers break out of the poverty trap, using their cultural strengths as equal partners in the great adventure of preserving and building a city.

The following objectives were set forth: to raise family income and reduce poverty and dependency, to raise the educational level, to strengthen family life and cultural institutions and to strengthen Puerto Rican organizational life.

Concurrent to training sessions for the board, I engaged staff and consultants for the study, as well as a staff for the South Bronx pilot program. A power struggle emerged that destroyed the potential for the PRCDP becoming a true community development project. In my opinion, the project that continued became a network of social service entities. Several local leadership bases were formed and continue to this day, but the Bronx did not develop the economic infrastructure that the proposal set forth. Over time, the conflict became defined as an ideological fight between a professionally-based movement and a grass-roots movement. I never agreed that it was an ideological struggle, only one over the control of funds. The members of the Forum were naive about the nature of power, and the large amount of money that was to be made available attracted a new breed of leaders that took over our project. The federal requirement for "maximum feasible participation" of the poor at all levels of the project, which led us to have a board of sixty-seven members, made the structure cumbersome and doomed to failure. We did not know why and with what motives other leaders of the Puerto Rican community were working against us, but they were using the Commonwealth office of the government of Puerto Rico in the city to oppose us. The Commonwealth engaged consultants to prepare a proposal to secure poverty funds before we could complete our proposal. Some of these leaders were inside our PRCDP board and had access to our work and the progress of our proposal. All of these factors complicated the relationships and power dynamics in our community. Racial tensions between the groups vying for monies were used by the city's political leaders effectively to guarantee that our efforts would not succeed. Actually, what we faced was also occurring elsewhere around the country. The large sums of money created a completely different model of work. The big poverty programs and the poverty bosses were ushered in.

The PRCDP had both its successes and failures. We succeeded in that we brought together the existing Puerto Rican community organizations and the most respected religious, social, intellectual, educational, business, labor, cultural, and political leaders of our community to study poverty and to design possible approaches to combat that poverty. We succeeded in that we were able to organize persons from multiple and diverse community groups, and to create a project board. We also were able to bring together a team of professionals, paraprofessionals, consultants, and supportive staff to mount a pilot project. This experience taught us about the chronic and destructive conditions in which the majority of Puerto Rican families in New York City were living. The most devastating fact that we uncovered was that the scenario of chronic poverty would continue for years to come because the poorest families had many children. The study presented a comprehensive picture of the conditions of the Puerto Rican community in New York in 1964, and is still valid.

Where we failed miserably was in recognizing the early signals of the coming power play. We did not understand the degree of deception that would take place and the extent to which some of our leaders would go to obtain money and power. The emerging power play came as a reaction to our effort to duplicate the model of the HARY-OU-ACT. This model necessitated that we bring together the leaders of "hometown groups" (municipalities in Puerto Rico) in the Bronx. These leaders included Ramón Vélez, Monserrate Flores, and others who were candidates for political positions; a group coalescing around the "hometown groups" based in El Barrio that included labor organizer Gerena Valentín, and other loosely affiliated Brooklyn groups relating to the Commonwealth and to the Democratic Party in Brooklyn; and others from religious and community-based groups. This mixture of interests and motivations would prove to be explosive.

We in the Forum had done our political homework with the Democratic politicians in Washington, D.C. We had a promise of $4 million. The black community had already received $40 million for its project. We were rushing to meet the deadline for funding before the direction of the War on Poverty would be moved from Washington, D.C., to city and state political control.

In this process, I learned two things that caused the final break of the Forum from the PRCDP's board. First, a former classmate of mine from the white community called to inform me that he had been hired by the Commonwealth to write a proposal for funding from the War on Poverty, a proposal that would compete with ours. He was calling me because he believed that he had an ethical responsibility to deal honestly with me as a professional colleague. Our staff continued to work at backbreaking speed to present the proposal prior to the deadline. However, when it was completed and presented to the board of PRCDP, a very odd thing occurred: At two consecutive meetings, we, the staff, could not obtain board approval for the proposal. Arguments at the meetings developed, and people almost ended up hitting one another with chairs. This was done to scare the female members of the board, and it worked. The women left the meetings. Consequently, no quorum was possible at the time of the vote on the proposal. Prior to the third meeting and the effort to obtain approval for the proposal, I accidentally ran into one of the women who was on the board. Very vocal and aggressive, she asked me if I was going to the afternoon planning meeting at Mobilization for Youth. She urged me to attend, saying that at this meeting we would plan what would happen at the

PRCDP board that evening. It was very obvious that she was concerned that I attend so that I could cooperate with the decision that would be taken to interfere with the evening meeting. She also informed me that these planning sessions had been held before every board meeting, and she had not seen me in attendance. I understood clearly at this point that there had been an organized effort by some members of the PRCDP board to sabotage our work and prevent the Forum proposal from receiving any money from the War on Poverty. Further, it became very clear that members of the PRCDP board, persons within our own community, were the organizers of the sabotage.

That afternoon, I called the president of the PRCDP board, and between the two of us, we called an emergency meeting hours before the evening PRCDP board meeting. The decision taken by the Puerto Rican Forum, ASPIRA, and others angry at the information known to us, was that we would resign en masse from the PRCDP board.

That evening, we announced our resignations. Twenty-seven members, out of a board of sixty-seven, resigned that evening. The members that left were mostly the organized professional agencies. Those who remained on the board were the community organizations, some churches, and some political leaders. Our resignations left the remaining group to have governance and control over the use of the proposal to request funds and the eventual implementation of the community development project.

The New York Times published three articles on the struggle in the PRCDP on March 4, March 16, and March 20, 1965. On March 4, *The New York Times* reported on the breakdown of the board: "A spokesman for the Anti-Poverty Operations Board said last night that it hoped to announce a city community action project, including Puerto Rican programs, within the next two weeks. 'The board,' he said, 'has assigned Joseph Morales, a former Puerto Rican government community organizer, to develop a Puerto Rican program.'"

The news of the decision made by the Anti-Poverty Operations Board was understood by the Puerto Rican Forum as a violation of the very essence and commitment implied in the phrase "maximum participation of the poor." The document, study, and proposal that the PRCDP had worked on was the product of the participation of our entire community as represented by the board. The study and the proposal was then set aside, and a staff person was hired to prepare and implement a "Puerto Rican program" that was different. The conclusion we drew was that the federal funds designated to combat poverty would be distributed by the political machine of the local government, insuring its hold on power. The new mechanism would be secured by the War on Poverty city agency and the traditional patronage system.

Following this decision, many times I have pondered whether our decision to resign the leadership of the Community Development Project was a mistake. I always conclude that it was the best decision, although it meant that our study and the approaches we designed were disregarded. Even now when I read the document, I believe that the plan was very good and that we might have greatly changed the nature of the powerlessness that exists for our people in the city today.

The work of the Puerto Rican Forum cannot be understood unless one understands its mission to create institutions to deal with problems that the Puerto Rican community of New York City encountered in obtaining employment, raising families, acquiring education, and in receiving the rights and resources that all citizens should receive. The Puerto Rican Forum had developed a series of specific objectives to accomplish its mission. One of the most important was the development of a leadership of commitment that would involve itself in the work of identifying community problems and devising strategies for solutions. Another important objective was to identify the knowledge and information on Puerto Rican history and on facts about Puerto Ricans and their culture to disseminate in our community and to others. The Forum also had commitments to help our people acquire work skills commensurate with obtaining well-paid employment and to teach our people the necessary skills to establish business enterprises.

I participated in the creation of very exciting and successful projects during my tenure with the Forum. After the work in completing the poverty study and program, the Forum engaged me as a consultant to develop a project called the Agency for Business and Career Development (ABCD). This was an idea that I conceived for reaching various segments of our community. The business component of the project was directed to men and women entrepreneurs who had existing businesses but who needed capital and/or increased management and administration skills to make their businesses more successful. The career aspect of the project was directed toward improving the employment of workers in selected fields and upgrading their language skills and performance to open up opportunities for their advancement and promotion. The basic idea was to create a ladder of access where current employees moved up, thus opening the door for new entrants. This program, named Basic Occupational Language Training (BOLT), was designed by a creative linguist, Ana Zentella, and me. Zentella not only worked on the teaching methodology, but also designed the construction of a mobile teaching bus that could be taken to workers' locations. Ana identified the language needed for the workers to move to a higher paying job once they had mastered the English language and the new job requirements. This program was very successful among busboys wanting to become waiters, hospital attendants wishing to become lab technicians, housing guards preparing to become supervisors. Grants were secured from the U.S. Department of Labor to operate the program, and because of its success, it was used to train Puerto Ricans, Chinese, and other populations coming into the city.

In the entrepreneurship component of the program, we were able to obtain a grant from the Ford Foundation to establish a relationship with three New York City banks that would offer loans to small businesses that accepted training from the Forum. Through this program, services were offered to various types of businesses. Our most successful effort was helping to develop a cooperative of bodegas, beauty parlors, and restaurants under the leadership of Johnny Torres in 1968. Johnny Torres had conceived of and implemented a Puerto Rican instrument, La Metro, to buy and store collectively vegetables and other perishables. Under the leadership of Torres, the collective became a major business incubator in the South Bronx.

In fulfilling its commitment to educate our people about their history and the culture of the island of Puerto Rico, the Forum sponsored weekend courses taught by faculty members from the University of

Puerto Rico. The courses were open to Puerto Rican adults, the youth of ASPIRA, social workers, teachers, agency executives, and heads of city departments. We conducted studies and compiled information that was not previously known: the number of Puerto Rican teachers and other personnel employed in the school system, the total number of Puerto Rican personnel in city and state agencies, etc.

Learning the History of My Country While in Exile

As I worked in my community, I gave of my intelligence, skills, and resources, but I also learned. There were many opportunities to gain new knowledge and skills. I also learned about the country of my birth and its relationship to the United States. It is the strangest realization to discover that I learned about the history of Puerto Rico while living in New York City. In 1964, while ASPIRA was a program of the Puerto Rican Forum, the Forum decided to offer a series of Saturday sessions on the history of Puerto Rico. In order to offer these sessions, the decision was made to bring in a professor from the University of Puerto Rico to teach the history and culture of Puerto Rico. We asked Dr. Luis Nieves Falcón to fly in on Friday nights to offer the course on Saturday mornings and afternoons. The course was announced to the Puerto Rican community in general and specifically to teachers and other professionals who would be interested in learning about Puerto Rico. Of course, the first targeted audience was the youth in the ASPIRA clubs. The response was great.

While we were committed to ASPIRA club members learning about the history of Puerto Rico, I realized that I, too, needed the course. In my high school and university studies, I had never had a course on the history of Puerto Rico. Oddly enough, this is true of most Puerto Ricans of my generation educated on the island. Unless you had gone out of your way to read independently, this information was not available because the schools did not offer it. In my own life, I had known from my grandmother's constant stories that there had been a bombing of San Juan by the American navy and that people had run out of the city into the wilderness. The wilderness was then Puerta de Tierra. As a child, I had also learned of the tale of a young Taíno native of the island who ran into the sea trying to escape the

Spanish soldiers. He preferred to run into the sea rather than be captured, and his dog had turned to stone waiting for him. This was a legend that we all read in a book called *Leyendas*, by Cayetano Coll y Toste. I do not remember how I came to read this book, but I always felt reverence when I would see the rock that represented the dog in the area where the ocean meets Laguna Condado. There were always teachers who would go out of their way to bring in some history, but it was not part of the formal lessons because there was no class called the "History of Puerto Rico."

From these bits and pieces, I learned that the island was discovered by Columbus, and Columbus was assisted by Queen Isabela in making his voyages to the New World, and that the original inhabitants of the Island, the Taínos, were constantly attacked by other peoples of the island of Cuba, the Caribes, who supposedly were cannibals and would attack the island of Puerto Rico to capture young maidens and eat Taíno men. I have never been able to ascertain the truthfulness of this information about the Caribes.

I do not really know how I got this information, but these bits were integrated into my learning at some point during elementary school. I learned as an adult living in New York that we had acquired a lot of misinformation. Reading the newspapers in Puerto Rico, one would also acquire pieces of information about history, such as the fact that there was a pirate named Cofresí who came from the town of Cabo Rojo. As a child, I also knew about various points where Columbus was supposed to have landed in 1493. We knew from the celebration of the various holidays that Columbus had left Spain from the port of Palos in three ships and crossed the Atlantic Ocean after many days of hardship, discovering a new world on his first voyage. On his second voyage, he discovered the island of Puerto Rico that was called Borinquen by the island inhabitants, whom the Spaniards called "Indians." There was no knowledge or discussion, as far as I recall, about Africans being brought to the island, but I knew that one of our holidays was called the "Abolition of Slavery." We knew that there were some famous men who had been abolitionists, Segundo Ruiz-Belvis and Ramón Emeterio Betances.

All of the information given to us was not integrated into the history of our country. However, while I lived at my grandmother's house in Barrio Obrero, I had a personal experience related to the Ponce Massacre.

Many people commented on these events, but we, as children, were asked to leave the discussion area. My brother would say that maybe one day he would march in the plaza with the soldiers. I thought that this idea was very exciting, but I could not march, being a female. No one ever explained why the people who marched in Ponce were killed or who killed them.

Acquiring a full picture of the history of my country was the result of the courses offered in New York every Saturday by Dr. Luis Nieves Falcón. I still keep copies of the materials that he distributed.

The courses of Dr. Falcón became a traditional offering that the Puerto Rican Forum provided the community. Also invited to give seminars were other New York-based professors, including Dr. María Teresa Babín, Dr. Carmen Marrero, and Dr. Diana Ramírez de Arellano. The Puerto Rican Forum had made the decision that we needed to return these professionals and their knowledge to the service of the community and get them to participate in the development of our young people. We thought that we should offer them the opportunity to be of service to Puerto Rican New Yorkers. The professors were people who had come from the island and had gotten positions because of their education and expertise as writers, historians, and so on. The Forum had actively sought the names, addresses, and positions of Puerto Rican professionals in the city. We later added to our roster the names of physicians, engineers, judges, and other professionals, and asked them to become mentors to our youth. We would offer them orientation about our youth and about the problems faced by the community. They often did not know much about the specific problems that our community was facing in New York, but we had little trouble in soliciting their aid. We received a warm response from these people, and began to form a network of mentors who donated time and money to our efforts. This network became a very important part of the program of ASPIRA. Many scholars and other professionals would join us over the years.

The courses in Puerto Rican history became a discovery of our own history and our country. The courses covered both history and culture, and represented an exceptional learning experience for us. They also represented an excellent political perspective. The knowledge that the government of Puerto Rico had encouraged a migration of its people to the States made me want to uncover the results of such an act. I began to develop in ASPIRA a repository of information on the situation of Puerto Rican students in New York high schools. One of the members of our board, Eugene Calderón, who was working for the New York City Board of Education, began to provide us with information we had never heard about the retention rates of Puerto Ricans from elementary school through postsecondary school. The information was alarming and became a central piece for the document that was later presented to the War on Poverty for establishing the Puerto Rico Community Development Project.

My grandmother, Luisa
Acosta de Pantoja, in
1949.

My mother, Alejandrina Pantoja,
in 1948.

My graduation from Columbia University.

My home in Calle Sol in Puerto Rico.

Retreat in St. Helena with students from The Graduate School with Dr. Perry and me.

Aspira Club Federation (ACF) at a meeting with me, Luis Nuñez, and Carmen Morales.

Members of the Hispanic Young Adult Association (HYAA) *circa* 1950.

Dr. Wilhelmina Perry and I standing in front of the building of the
Graduate School for Community Development

To Antonia Pantoja

President Bill Clinton awards me the Presidential Medal of Freedom.

Fifth Part

Leadership in the Overall Society
(1965–1969)

Living in the city for twenty or more years, I had acquired a number of friends and acquaintances, which offered me the opportunity to function on various levels and circles of the city. My life was rich in experiences related to my work in the Puerto Rican community, the social work, education, and fundraising spheres of the city. I also enjoyed the arts, music, cultural activities, political debates, and social gatherings, as well as the foods, theater, ballet, symphony, and friends offered by the many cultures of New York. My participation in the life of the city also included party politics. These activities provided me with contacts who did not necessarily know one another and gave me opportunities for constant learning and growing. I was never bored, but I missed the companionship and love of a special person with whom I could share my life. This void continued to be present for many years. I lived a busy and full life that missed the realization of intimacy, passion, and commitment to and with another person.

A University Professor

One day, I cannot remember exactly when, I received a letter inviting me to consider teaching at the Columbia School of Social Work. The letter invited me to a meeting with the dean and other professors to discuss the offer of a position in the community organization program. I accepted the position. The offer came in the late spring, so I spent the summer reading and preparing course work for my teaching in the coming autumn. I took a driving trip across the country with my friend Barbara Blourock to San Francisco and back to New York City. After I returned, I devoted my time to reading and putting my life in order before beginning this new teaching assignment.

Once I had begun the new job, I found myself being addressed as "Professor" Pantoja. I most certainly did not wish to be heard saying that I was impressed by being a professor. It is all right to say it here, because many years have gone by. But I was impressed with being called a professor. I suddenly realized that although I had become a New Yorker before, it was not this kind of New Yorker. I now could say that I had arrived! I had reached one of the professions of highest prestige in the country: faculty member at Columbia University. However, I did not have the proper attitude. Frankly, I was immensely unhappy and felt empty. I felt alone and sorry that I had left ASPIRA. I was teaching at the school where my faculty advisor had said "over my dead body will you be allowed to graduate with a community organization concentration." Now, I was a faculty member teaching in the community organization program. Many times, I was tempted to meet with him to remind him, but I thought it would not be a good thing to do.

The Columbia University School of Social Work was located in the Carnegie Mansion on Fifth Avenue and 91st Street. It felt like a mausoleum. The faculty came in to teach and left in a hurry to their respective consultations. They were not very friendly, with the exception of my colleagues in the community organization program. I rarely spoke with anyone. Sometimes the five faculty in our program happened to meet in the hall or in each other's offices. They were George Braeger, Simon Slavin, Preston Wilcox, James Hacker, and me. Two were black, two were Jewish, and I was the only Puerto Rican. I looked forward to our faculty meetings. The chairperson, Sy, wanted to develop a program with a sound theoretical base. He provoked and encouraged open discussions on the problems we encountered within the profession.

The year that I joined the faculty, we began an effort to identify the concepts that underlie our methods. We began by identifying how community organization differed from casework and group work. We reached agreement that at least community organization was a method to organize people. But what was missing? Organize people to what end? How do we arrive at the decision to organize people? Provoked by the faculty meetings, I designed a visual idea of my understanding of why and how community organizers work with communities. This design later became my conceptualization of community development and would become the basic idea for creating a freestanding graduate school in San Diego, California. The end we were pursuing was social change: change of the community and of the society. This had never been articulated as an accepted objective of the profession.

In my own understanding of things, through experiences, study, and professional development, I knew that the society in which we lived was wrong. Experiences in my own community had clearly and forcefully demonstrated to me that poor and excluded communities could pull themselves out of the condition of poverty if the institutions of the society offered them the services, resources, education, and skills to become productive members. I knew that the members of these communities were considered the problem and accused of creating the ills that they suffered; the society and its institutions absolved themselves of any responsibility for creating the problems. I know that because I am a member of one of these communities.

I soon found out that being a professor at Columbia University brought many opportunities beyond the rewards of teaching. I had an opportunity to engage in activities that involved major policymaking and decision-making in the city. None of my colleagues ever acknowledged my contributions.

A Delegate to the New York State Constitutional Convention

The first "outside" opportunity I received was my election to become a delegate-at-large to the 1967 New York State Constitutional Convention. Our task was to write a new constitution for New York. This happened in a very amazing way. One day as I arrived home from the university, a man's voice told me on the telephone that the six o'clock news would announce my election as a delegate-at-large for New York City to the convention. I had received the support of both the Democratic and Liberal Parties. The caller identified himself as Robert Kennedy and he asked if I would accept the appointment. The time was 4:00 P.M. I asked how the appointment had come about. He rapidly explained that I was selected by the two parties as the best person from the Puerto Rican community and because I was a social worker teaching at the Columbia School of Social Work. I said that I wished I had been consulted or had known of the position to have the opportunity to seek advice from members of my community whom I trusted. He said that I should call him back after my consultation. He was at the Carlyle Hotel.

I spoke to Paco Trilla, a friend whose judgment I trusted. Paco had been the president of the board of most of the institutions that I had helped create. We respected each other's opinion. Paco told me that I should accept because, in that position, I could bear my views and experiences about the conditions of the poor, especially about the poverty and discrimination faced by Puerto Ricans. He also emphasized that my presence among these policymakers and political leaders would introduce them to a kind of Puerto Rican they had never met.

I decided to accept, but before I could return the call to Bobby Kennedy, the news had already announced my selection. Speaking later to other people who knew Bobby Kennedy, I was told that he was like that. He got his way with people. "Well!" I thought I did not like to be manipulated that way, but this act of his gave me a tremendous opportunity to participate in the policymaking arena in an influential manner, changing the document that influenced the decisions to be made by legislators.

The 1967 convention was called to change a document that had become obsolete; it needed to provide guidelines for legislating and governing the most complicated and fastest-growing city and state. However, some politicians were interested only in changes that benefited their political designs.

A number of delegates from the black and Puerto Rican communities formed a rebel group that would meet informally after each legislative session to discuss issues that affected our respective communities and to arrive at voting positions that we considered just and beneficial for our people. We had realized, by counting votes, that we were a deciding vote needed by the Liberal and Democratic Party delegates to secure victory from the Republicans on the heavily discussed articles of the constitution. One of these articles was the Blaine Amendment, which prohibited the use of public funds for religious institutions or activities. This amendment had interfered with decisions passed by the state legislature to assign funds to parochial schools. The call to a convention that year had the intention of eliminating the Blaine Amendment. Our minority caucus decided we would use the Blaine issue to bargain for articles that we wanted passed, such as for economic development, job creation, and labor unions. When the vote for the Blaine Amendment was announced, we left Albany so we could not be located. The president of the convention, a democratic lawyer from Brooklyn, had a reputation as a strong politician who used high-handed methods to get a vote to go his way. He sent state police to get us back to vote. The Puerto Rican delegates had gone to Puerto Rico, and it was necessary for the police to locate us at hotels and family homes. This was Friday, and we were ordered to return for a vote on Monday.

Once we were back, a special caucus meeting of Democrats and Liberals was called by the president of the convention. I had never participated in a caucus meeting, so I was very surprised and apprehensive when the assistants to the president of the convention locked the doors of the room so that no one would leave or enter the room. Attendance was called, and the president explained the purpose of the caucus. He requested that those present back him in passing the proposal that he would present to the convention on the Blaine Amendment. He went on to say that he was a generous fellow who remembered those who helped him win his battles, and he had a good memory for those who opposed him. Our minority delegation eyed each other to remind ourselves of our agreement. We had sent a message to the president that we were interested in the passage of our two issues: one on economic development and the other on labor unions. No message came back to us during the caucus or afterward. We held firm in our decision to vote negatively. The vote to poll delegates was taken many times with threats and admonitions thrown at us. Individual meetings would continue—sometimes with the president, other times with small groups of delegates. For a while, the caucus seemed to have no end. The pressure tactics increased with loud voices presenting persuasive reasons and veiled threats of harm.

We waited for the message from the president that he would accept our two measures favoring economic development and labor unions. We later learned that a message had been sent back from the president, but that it had never been delivered to us. We never learned what the answer was or why the messenger never returned the answer to us. We never forgave the member-delegate who had decided not to bring back the message. He later ran for office in the city and did not receive our support.

The caucus ended, and we returned to the open meeting where the Republicans had been waiting for hours. The vote on the Blaine Amendment was called, and it lost with the support of our vote against it. I had never participated in a closed caucus or had an experience of this kind. The experience was menacing, nerve-racking, and frightening. Thinking about it now, I do not know what I was afraid of. I can only say that the occasion represented a raw and direct confrontation with the power of this country through its political processes.

Once the convention had ended, I realized that it was truly an empowering and rewarding experience for us, a small group of minority representatives. We had stuck together in the face of strong and almost dangerous threats. That weekend, the president invited all of the delegates to dinner. He made a point to speak in a friendly manner to our group of delegates. In the end, the convention lost completely as the voters of New York defeated the new constitution when it was presented for a vote. This experience offered me a small taste of what goes on in political battles. I did not like it. I stayed away from this arena even when offered a specific opportunity. In a meeting Robert Kennedy called with a group of us young Puerto Ricans to meet with him on one of his visits to the Hotel Carlyle, he asked me to run for a position in the Upper West Side under the banner of the reform Democrats. He tried very hard to convince me that this was a good road to take. I declined very emphatically. Constance Motley was then supported as the candidate, and she won.

Many of the members of my group were critical of my decision and could not understand why I declined. Now, I can speak about what I never told them. The life of a political candidate is one of grave pressure under the attack of enemies whom one does not even know. I did not want my private life examined and exposed to public scrutiny. I did not know who my father was, and I feared that there might be public information that would hurt my mother. Also, I had never married. I had led a bohemian life in my early years, and since then, I had had a number of female companions. I felt that all these things could have been the subject of personal attacks because I knew that political campaigns use low tactics. These are the reasons why I declined the offer to run for public office.

During my work as a delegate to the Constitutional Convention, I was befriended by persons whom I would have never known in the city. I shared my office in Albany with Marietta Tree, an active member of the Democratic Party. Many times, upon returning to the city, she asked me to ride with her in her chauffeur-driven Rolls Royce. In the beginning, I flew into Albany with all the other delegates selected by Kennedy. We flew in the *Caroline,* the Kennedys' plane. Marietta Tree also suggested that we pool our stipend so that we could do more with the money. She agreed that I hire a young Puerto Rican to organize and orient a group of youth into the political processes, to observe the sessions, and to meet and talk with the delegates. I hired Joe Aguayo, who was then a young student and consultant at the Puerto Rican Forum. He and I organized a group that we called the Puerto Rican Institute for Political Participation (PRIPP). PRIPP was composed of Puerto Rican youth in college and high school. The purpose of the group was to experience the political process and meet some of the political leaders of the city at work. The group continued to exist after the convention ended, housed in the Puerto Rican Forum. Many of its members became active in politics.

I was really a New Yorker now! But I was very different from the New Yorker who had lived and socialized with young artists and conscientious objectors who would not go to war, with the veterans of the Lincoln Brigade, and with the merchant marines who smuggled arms to the fighters for a Jewish homeland. Now, I was a member of the established leadership of the city. How did this happen? I was being offered access into this new world of "power brokers." I did not accept becoming this kind of New Yorker. I was an outspoken advocate for the

rights of our community, and I spoke at public forums expressing my
views and opinions. I had elected and taken the road to becoming a
spokesperson for my excluded community. My own position was
becoming clearer in my own head and clarified in the public arena. I
agreed to teach a course on community organizing at the New School
for Social Research. My students were employed men and women volunteers who were involved in organizing projects to combat abuses of
citizens' rights. Students in the course received no grades. The course
required reading and a term paper. The students read avidly and
brought to me materials relevant to the topics of the class. I can say that
we truly learned from each other. I fully enjoyed the experience.

A Member of Mayor Lindsay's Bundy Blue Ribbon Panel

When the Constitutional Convention ended its work, I was named
by Mayor Lindsay to be a member of the Bundy Blue Ribbon Panel
to design a legal process for decentralizing the New York City Board
of Education. This panel was a response to very strong criticism raised
against the board by parents, teachers, educational leaders, scholars,
press, and strong citywide parents' associations. The panel was
presided over by McGeorge Bundy, the president of the Ford Foundation. Other members of the panel were: Alfred Giardino, president of
the Board of Education; Michael Sviridoff, head of the city's Human
Resources Administration; Francis Keppel, president of General
Learning Corporation and former U.S. Commissioner of Education;
and Benetta Washington, head of the Women's Job Corps and former
high school principal.

Benetta, who was black, and I represented our respective communities. We had a group of working consultants to help us with the
facts about the historical life of the board and about the student population, efforts at integration, and the necessary legislative requirements to decentralize the board. The plan was to replace the central
board by creating local district boards that would include teachers and
parents. Compared to the work of the Constitutional Convention, this
task was far easier. We finished our report and handed the mayor our
plan of decentralization into district offices, giving power to parents,
teachers, administrators, and residents of the area, as members of dis-

trict boards.

The work of the panel became heavy with evening meetings full of anger and disagreement among all affected parties. The hostility of members of some groups was intense, and Benetta and I carried a larger responsibility because of our experience in working in communities. School administrators did not want to share power with teachers. Teachers did not want to share power with parents. No one wanted students to participate in the new local boards. The power dynamics were very clear. Those who had always controlled decision-making in the schools did not want to share power with others.

After many battles fought in meetings at the Board of Education, in the state legislature, and later in the courts, a law was approved to divest the central Board of Education of full power over the schools of the city. Although the minority members of the panel did not completely secure all the changes that we wanted, we achieved the right to divide the city into small school districts. A district board composed of community members and professionals would administer the budget, hire and evaluate teachers, and work with a district superintendent. We were unable to secure a local district that would include student representation and/or allow only parents of students (in the school) to be elected to the local boards.

While I taught at the School of Social Work and the New School and participated in the convention and the panel, I continued to offer the Puerto Rican Forum voluntary time. That year, I reached my maximum income capacity. The combined income placed me in a new tax bracket. I was able to purchase land in Puerto Rico along with other young Puerto Ricans. In this way, I felt that we could have a voice in the future affairs of our country.

The winter of 1968 was a bitterly cold one. I had become increasingly susceptible to the cold weather. My asthma attacks were becoming very acute at night. Even with medication, it was impossible to control the attacks at night and to recuperate in the morning. My busy schedule had exhausted me.

Reflections and Ruminations

The four years of my life that propelled me from ASPIRA to a pro-

fessorship at Columbia University, to participating in the writing of a
new constitution for the state of New York, to planning the decentralization of the Board of Education of the city of New York, and to teaching at the New School for Social Research almost killed me by deplet-
ing my physical resources. I had left ASPIRA, and, frankly, my work
output had been significantly reduced. I looked forward to new and
challenging opportunities. I was moving into a new arena of functioning, and I was learning firsthand about the making of public policy.

The education that I had given up in rejecting the Fulbright Scholarship was now a real-life experience, in which I was observing firsthand the white male leadership of the city and state. I was able to cor-
roborate directly that our society was based on our policy decisions
that created inequality. I confirmed it when I tried to promote the idea
that the public school system had to be expanded to include the four
years of college and also when I argued for the assigning of funds to
corporations that would stay in or return to the crumbling inner cities.
My ideas were supported by writers and scholars who had participated in the debates to create a public school system that would educate
all students up to high school. These advocates believed in the public
school system as the foundation of a democratic society. The arguments now opposing the inclusion of four years of college were the
same arguments that had been used to fight against high school as a
part of a public system. The same group of elected officials and leaders of the state of New York opposed the idea of incentives for attract-
ing corporations to inner cities through the provision of funds for the
training of unemployed men and women who would become skilled
employees of these and other companies.

As the chairperson of the subcommittee on education and the subcommittee on economic development of the convention, I was also
able to read and understand the historical processes used to develop
the legislation that established the public school system. I read about
the new ideas being proposed by thinkers in Europe, who were developing new approaches to city planning, the training of workers, and
the revitalization of urban centers. In the United States, some archi-
tects were proposing new approaches for the mixed use of physical
structures that would bring together commercial, industrial, housing,

and services, in planned buildings.

I read Jane Jacobs's discussions about making more humane and livable cities. In my own mind, I was considering the measures that could be taken to address the deterioration and destruction of our urban communities. I learned how to mobilize resources and utilize political power to affect policy decisions. The new ideas proposed by the subcommittees were not voted for inclusion by the delegates into the new articles for the constitution. The new constitution was also not accepted by the voters of New York State. The voters considered the amendment a strategy to bring public funds to parochial schools. Such a position was opposed by non-Catholic voters.

Although we were not successful, I felt satisfied that I had tested and proven myself in a new arena controlled by political heavyweights. I was learning from others while teaching myself. I was expanding the education that I had received in my own professional training, and I was providing learning opportunities for Puerto Rican young adults. I was formulating and testing theories of power and pedagogy that would form the foundation for my future work. My world was expanding. I was stimulated and motivated by the experiences. Later, in the struggles on the panel to decentralize the schools, the fights were much easier for me. I learned and came to understand more. I was able to see clearly the ways in which various interest groups of the school bureaucracy and the unions acted to protect their positions and turfs, frequently in ways detrimental to the needs of the children.

I began to see the new professional leaders of our community, who had emerged from the convention, moving into newly accessible administrative positions in city agencies and the political party, but they had little or no understanding of the exclusion and disenfranchisement of nonwhite people in the society. They were new leaders who had not come by their positions through involvement with the Puerto Rican community, and therefore, they owed allegiance to the majority community and not to us. I continued to call for the development of a leadership of ethical commitment, but the response that I usually received was that I was a naive social worker or educator who did not understand "how one gets to the top."

When I completed this work and returned to consulting for the

Puerto Rican Forum, I successfully used the knowledge that I had learned about coalition-building to establish an economic development program that had linkages with the Jewish and black communities. These new programs pooled resources, shared information and knowledge, and ultimately helped to open doors that we Puerto Ricans could not have entered alone. The institutions were the banks, universities, and high-level consultant groups.

After this period of teaching and working in the convention, I became ill. Years later, I learned of my pattern of plunging into work to the point of becoming ill. My own compulsiveness, the urgency to accomplish social change, and my personal feelings of loneliness, would drive me to occupy every moment with work. After several such illnesses, and while living in California, I was forced to deal with this problem and correct my manner of functioning.

Today is the ninth day of the month of March in the year 2000. I find myself writing a book on my life. I just realized that this is a very big enterprise that I have undertaken. It means that I will be writing the story of my seventy-eight years on this earth. This is a scary thought, but I have undertaken larger projects before and I have never been frightened by them. Thinking very seriously, I am impressed by the enormity of the work, but I am not really frightened.

Looking back at those seventy-eight years, I can see that I have always been in the process of working on a project. In Puerto Rico, my first project was to learn how it might be possible to attend the university. Later, it was how to get a teaching appointment in the mountains of my country. Much later, the project was how to leave the island. Once in New York, I found myself preoccupied with the project of returning to school for a degree. Once I had achieved two degrees, I embarked on the larger and more complicated projects of organizing groups of young Puerto Ricans and establishing institutions to serve people. From that point on, I had a definite intent of finding ways to change social and economic conditions I considered harmful to people and to change human conditions that permitted and accepted these. Once a project was achieved, I moved on to another enterprise. I have often questioned myself about my constant engagement in new projects and building new institutions. Will I ever stop? Will I ever stay in one institution, where I can work and earn a livelihood? I know that I am not driven by the need to earn money because what I do does not bring large remuneration. I do not believe that personal fame is my motivation. I am a person who has experienced great pride in testing my intelligence and capacity to be productive to the fullest measure. This seems more at the root of this constant activity. The end of my self-analysis has given me satisfying insights into this aspect of my personality. I have concluded that I am motivated by a desire to be remembered as a person who has spent her life trying to improve the conditions and life chances of people in my community who do not enjoy the rights or the respect of other citizens in the society. I wish to be remembered as a person who has lived according to her philosophy, a person who is not a fake. In the end, if I am not satisfied by these answers, I can always fall back on what my grandmother used to say: "She is a child born with a special destiny!"

Over the years, I and others have made great contributions to improving life in the city of New York. There is no place in this city where the knowledge of our contributions is recorded. My book must tell the story of our contributions, not because we need praise for ourselves, but because as an immigrant group, we have succeeded in making a contribution to this city and the country, in spite of the obstacles and oppression placed on us by the society. Remember, we were organizing these programs and services before poverty monies were dispensed, and even when poverty monies were dispensed, we worked outside of these handouts. We have been a creative immigrant group trying to lift ourselves from the destructive, dependent role assigned to nonwhite, poor citizens of the city and the country.

If you consider that the largest wave of Puerto Ricans came to New York starting in 1945, our group has been in the city for only fifty-five years. During these fifty-five years, we who came without the knowledge of English, with few skills and no economic resources, have been able to accomplish many important projects and build many institutions. We have educated a leadership that has been instrumental in helping our group to obtain our rights; we have taken a case to the Supreme Court to force the Board of Education to teach children in two languages; we have established an accredited institution of higher education; we have elected persons to City Council, state senators, representatives in Congress. I believe that other New Yorkers evaluate our situation using standards that only find failure and poverty. Considering that we came to this country with many odds against us, I believe that we have done well in a short period of time, given the realities that we faced as an immigrant group of nonwhite people coming from a country that had been colonized by the United States.

Sixth Part

Return to Puerto Rico and Return to New York (1969–1983)

Returning Home

On an extremely cold morning in January 1969, my sister Lydia, who still lived in New York City and liked to take care of me when I needed her, accompanied me to Kennedy Airport to move to Puerto Rico. Most of my belongings had been packed by her and sent ahead, so that I only carried a suitcase. I felt very sick that morning and appreciated Lydia's loving care. A friend of mine, Barbara Blourock, joined us at the airport. She would go with me to Puerto Rico. I had decided to leave New York after I had spent many sleepless nights wheezing with asthma and being told by my doctor that I had to leave New York during the winter. The asthma was so bad that you could hear a whistling noise when I spoke.

The month of January had arrived with temperatures of ten to fifteen degrees below zero, so it was unbearable for me to walk in the cold to the subway or take a cab. Other, further complicating matters were that I could not sleep in my apartment with the heat on. This made it impossible for me to function. I made my decision and left in a hurry. My plan was to live in one of the houses that I had purchased in Old San Juan, the one that needed fewer repairs. The living expenses would be covered by my savings until the health insurance from the National Association of Social Workers arrived. I knew that the investigative process would take some time, but I was not prepared for the lack of response and denial of my claim. They denied the request based on their statement that I was "working in Puerto Rico." In anger and consternation, I wrote to my friend and lawyer, Harris Present, to represent my interests. Harris reported back to me that the insurance company informed him that their investigation had concluded that I left my house every morning to go to work. The investigator said that he verified this information by speaking with neighbors. Harris handled the situation in New York with the company when I explained what I did every morning. The insurance company eventually approved a small payment that would last less than three months. It was not enough to cover my needs, but since I did not pay rent, I thought that I could hold out until I was better and could hold a job.

During the first part of this period of adjustment and while I continued to be ill, I would get up early in the morning, eat breakfast, and ride the bus to the nearby beach in Puerta de Tierra, behind the old Hotel Normandie, now called the Radisson Hotel. I would sit on the sand, relax, take in the sun and fresh air, cleaning my lungs and feeling better every day. These were very effective medications that I combined with my doctor's medicines. I returned to the house by lunchtime, usually about 1:00 P.M. The full nights of sleep, the sun, and the warmth of the tropics began to work wonders, and my health improved. During the afternoon, I had the luxury of thinking and planning what I would do now that I was back in Puerto Rico. I had returned to Puerto Rico with many skills and the capacity to develop and administer a program or an agency.

Once I felt better, I began to identify opportunities for employment. Puerto Rico had elections, and it had a new governor whom I knew. Governor Luis Ferré was elected with the success of the New Progressive Party. This party was an evolution of the old Republicans, so it had a conservative approach and a strong ideology of having Puerto Rico become a state. It was a very closely knit and unimaginative group of politicians who used underhanded methods and had established a negative reputation.

Because I needed work, I applied for several positions in government agencies, but I did not succeed in even getting an interview, because the first requirement for a job was service to the party in past elections. This meant that I could not secure a job in the government, where most social service jobs in Puerto Rico are found. I would come home and fill out the paperwork to secure a telephone or to apply for a loan for the rehabilitation of one of the houses that I had bought. These were very difficult tasks, because ordinary people in government agencies cannot make the simplest decisions without asking their top supervisor to approve each level of decision-making. It took much work to receive approval for any part of the loan to get the work done on the house. Remembering the politics of Puerto Rico, I decided to obtain help from a well-connected colleague, the sister of Governor Luis Ferré. Sister Thomas Marie had been involved in several projects that I had done in New York City. I telephoned her in Ponce to ask for her help in finding a job with the administration in power. Her name had changed to Sister Isolina Ferré. She asked me to visit her in Ponce, and we had a very warm reconnecting. She promised to speak with Luis about me and my need for employment.

Don Luis Ferré had been the chairperson of ASPIRA's fundraising industrialists committed in Puerto Rico. Sister Isolina and I both agreed that he would remember me. She also suggested that I write some ideas for federally funded programs that could involve youth in projects of cleaning and beautifying cities.

I wrote an idea to recruit youths from poor families to work after school hours and on Saturdays, as well as unemployed youths to be trained as gardening crews in the streets of the major cities of Puerto Rico. I sent the document with a work plan to Sister Isolina, requesting that she send the materials from Washington to complete the proposals. I received the guidelines and application materials and completed the proposal and returned it to her. Sister Isolina requested that I visit her in Ponce, where we discussed an idea that she had for working in a very poor area of Ponce along the beach. We agreed that she would pay me for two days of work for the week and cover my travel expenses. She paid me to develop a project idea for working with youths who were identified by the schools, court, or police as being predelinquent. The program consisted of training young adults to work with the at-risk youths. The project also included creating a network of parents and community persons who would serve as advocates for the youths and keep them out of trouble.

I wrote the proposal to the Justice Department in Washington, D.C., and it was funded. I participated with Sister Isolina in recruiting the youths who would serve as the advocates. I did not continue to work with her in her beach community because the trips to Ponce and the stay for two days a week became too strenuous. The governor never answered me about the beautification proposal and never paid me for the proposal. Sister Isolina told me that the governor's advisors did not consider the discussion of my employment in a government agency favorably.

After this abortive trial at becoming a government employee, I proposed an idea to a friend, Dr. Luis Nieves Falcón, a professor at the University of Puerto Rico, to work with high school youth in the poor slums of San Juan. The program would organize youth clubs that would study the problems of their neighborhood and prepare a plan to solve the problems. The members of these groups would stay in high school, graduate, and continue postsecondary education. The proposal was presented to the Office of Education in Washington under the Talent Search program, and it received funding. The sponsoring board was a group that Dr. Nieves had organized, called Acción Social (Social Action), and the group had another project working with nursery-school children in housing projects. The Talent Search program required that the board demonstrate that it could raise at least one-third of the first-year budget, with the expectation that the project would become self-supporting the second year of activity. After much discussion, the board of Acción Social, composed of university professors and other professionals, decided that they could not raise the required matching funds for the project.

Nevertheless, the project, called Adelante Boricuas (Forward Boricuas) had become a success, with five groups in the San Juan vicinity and one group in Carolina. One hundred twenty youths were being served. With no guarantee of financial commitments from the board, I requested permission from the funding source in Washington to convert the project into an ASPIRA. The request was approved, and ASPIRA agreed to pay me a small consultant fee to convert the project, hire and train staff, organize and incorporate a board, and comply with the funding requirements to make the grant an ASPIRA grant.

This is how ASPIRA of Puerto Rico was founded.

The three houses that I owned in Puerto Rico had been part of a plan of my friends, New York Puerto Ricans, to assist in retaining land and houses in the hands of Puerto Ricans. Those of us who held jobs in New York purchased houses in San Juan, and land in the mountains and faraway towns. When I bought the land in El Yunque, Josie Nieves also bought land there. Yolanda Sánchez and her brother Nick bought land near the beach in Boquerón, a town on the beach in the southwest part of the island. After many months of trying to obtain a restoration loan for my house in old San Juan, I took a different approach that worked. I sold the two smaller houses and applied to a commercial bank, Banco Popular, for a restoration and purchase loan backed by the Economic Development Government Bank. This worked well because loan terms were more favorable with a commercial lender.

The restoration of the building that had once housed the Crafts Museum of the Institute of Culture turned into a beautiful product. My friend Barbara and I made it into a tourist guesthouse that we called La Casa del Sol because of its location on Sol Street. The house had an inner patio surrounded by bougainvilleas, purple and sun-yellow *canarias*, a large tropical flower. These climbing bushes draped the patio in a resplendent yellow glow in the daytime. All the small apartments opened onto this patio. We occupied a back apartment. All floors were the original marble, and all the rooms had tall ceilings supported by ironwood beams. We furnished the rooms in dark rattan chairs, tables, beds, and chests. Casa del Sol was a very beautiful place.

I sent brochures with photos to everyone whom I had ever worked with in the United States, and we arranged a plan to receive all "spillover guests" from the Hotel Convento nearby. The business was a great success. We had many guests from the States who stayed for weeks at a time. I was able to return the warmth of my dear friend Dr. Horne, when he visited me during his recuperation from a stroke. He spent a month as my guest.

Our business was so successful that we were breaking even and earning extra money by the sixth month after we opened. We employed a staff for cleaning and working around the guest house.

This plan posed problems because the staff was not dependable. Barbara and I would rush to clean and prepare apartments only hours before guests were to arrive from New York. Other problems affecting the business and our lives were the lack of telephone services, and the water and electricity shut-offs. It became very difficult for two women to operate and maintain the guest house. The burden on us of running the hotel became so difficult that we eventually decided to sell the business and move away from Puerto Rico.

Our decision to leave Puerto Rico had other considerations as well. I had secured an opportunity to teach a semester at the University of Puerto Rico School of Social Work. The class that I taught was on social change and how to work with people to help them change the problems that affect their communities. I was enjoying my class, because I had many matriculated students as well as others taking the class as non-registered students. Most of them were in the class to learn how to organize.

Although I earned very little for the class, $450 a semester, I wanted very much to continue teaching the course. My reputation grew, and students would wait outside my classroom to listen and to talk to me.

I had returned to Puerto Rico wearing sandals and donning a large Afro hairstyle. The students began to call me a "Black Panther," and I was quickly identified as a radical faculty person from New York. I enjoyed the class and the students' enthusiasm. However, at the end of the semester, it was best not to continue to teach. I found myself in a situation that confirmed for me that I could not live in Puerto Rico unless I abided to the traditional rules of conduct and "knew my place." As part of my teaching position, I was required to attend faculty meetings, even though I taught only one course. At my first faculty meeting, there was a discussion on evaluating projects, and I participated in the discussion. After a while, I felt that my participation wasn't being appreciated by the director. I had met the director of the school in New York through mutual friends. In addressing her in meetings, I called her by her first name. This was the first mistake that I committed. The second and more serious mistake was my full participation in a discussion, especially when I offered a definition of evaluation. My definition was in conflict with the school's definition, and it was met by a silence and a tense atmosphere, a clear annoyance to the director. After this contribution to the dialogue, I remained silent until the meeting ended. But I knew that it was too late; the damage had been done. When the meeting was over, I asked one of the oldest and most respected members of the faculty to permit me to ask her some questions about the meeting. I said, "Doña Carmen, tell me frankly if I am right. I think that I committed a serious mistake in the meeting, but I am not sure how." Doña Carmen said, "Do you really want to know what was considered wrong? I will tell you, frankly. Your first mistake was that you spoke at your first meeting. The second mistake was that you called the director by her first name. The third and most grievous mistake was that you disagreed with the director's idea and definition. There you are. Do you see now why your participation was not welcomed?"

I appreciated Doña Carmen's directness and honesty, and it was clear to me that I did not want to participate in a teaching community where the director was the only person who had legitimate views. I asked to speak with the director, and I informed her that I would not attend any more faculty meetings. I informed her that I would complete teaching the course, but I had no intention of returning once the semester ended. This act on my part ended all future possibilities for any relationship with the School of Social Work of the University of Puerto Rico.

The second event that made it impossible for me to stay in Puerto Rico happened soon after we had decided not to continue with the guest house. I formed a consulting firm, including three members from New York City. The members were Dr. Charles Bahn, a professor at Baruch College of the City University of New York, and Mr. Héctor Vásquez, the executive director of the Puerto Rican Forum, and Barbara Blourock. The firm was Pantoja Associates. We planned to compete for contracts in Puerto Rico and the United States. The purpose of the firm was to bring in some income because I was once again without a source of employment.

Our firm started with a proposal to evaluate Model Cities programs in Puerto Rico. After several weeks of waiting with no formal communication, one day I received a telephone call from my "insider" friend, who angrily said, "*Coño,* Toni, why did you call your corporation Pantoja Associates? You should have called it Smith Associates. They just announced the awarding of the contracts. I was present in the discussions of the proposals, and yours was the best, the most professionally presented, with a solid experience background in evaluation, but your corporation was Puerto Rican! The contract was awarded to an American company, a corporation from California."

Of course, we were very angry because Dr. Bahn was known for having conducted many evaluation programs of Model Cities programs in the United States. The firm selected had no such prior experience. My friend told me later that in the government of Puerto Rico, during the Ferré administration, American consulting firms were preferred to Puerto Rican ones.

After this happened, I found that I could work outside of Puerto Rico more easily than in Puerto Rico. I accepted contracts in Bogotá, Columbia, San Francisco, and San Diego. I decided that if I was going to be on an airplane to earn my livelihood, I might as well move back to the States. I had returned to my country, my place of birth, and I could not find work. Although I had proven myself many times over in my work stateside, in Puerto Rico, I was an outsider who did not know her place.

An important visit from a friend, Luis Álvarez, who was now a member of the board of directors of the Puerto Rican Forum, shook me from my unhappiness and feeling of being useless. Luis and I sat in the patio of Casa del Sol for an entire afternoon talking about my experiences in Puerto Rico. He made a remark at the beginning of our conversation that he repeated several times as we talked. He finally ended the visit in the evening at dinner by saying it again: "Toni, we New Yoricans need you. What are you doing here where they do not want you and do not appreciate who you are and the abilities that you have as an institution builder and a problem solver? Come to New York, and I will present a proposal for you to continue your work of institution-building in New York. Prepare a proposal for us to get back to where we left off."

After many telephone discussions and letters exchanged with

members of the board of the Puerto Rican Forum, I decided to write a proposal to establish a research center to be used by Puerto Ricans and non-Puerto Ricans who needed information and research that existed on Puerto Ricans. This was one of the institutions proposed in the Puerto Rican Community Development Project. The Forum accepted the idea during a meeting that I attended. It was presented to the Ford Foundation and was accepted for funding, based on the condition that we secure additional funds as their monies decreased. The decision was made to establish the Research Center in Washington, D.C., to serve the needs of communities in the Northeast and Spanish-speaking communities in Washington. The research center opened the possibility of approaching the Fund for the Improvement of Post-Secondary Education (FIPSE) in the Department of Education. With this good news, Barbara Blourock and I packed our belongings and the property of Casa del Sol for transportation to Washington, D.C.

In two-and-a-half years in Puerto Rico, from January 1969 to July 1971, I felt physically better and my asthma had improved, but my spirit was heavy from the discouraging contact with my country. The return was upsetting. I began to question my identity as a Puerto Rican, my love and appreciation for my culture. I wrote six pages on a yellow, legal-size pad, listing the reasons why I was once again leaving the island. I intended to be analytical and not emotional about my feelings. In July 1971, I boarded an American Airlines plane for my destination, Washington, D.C., where I had a house and a project waiting for me.

The second emigration from Puerto Rico was by airplane, not by boat, as was the first passage. This time the trip lacked the anticipation and romance of the first one. It was not the same to immigrate to New York as to immigrate to Washington, D.C.

A Research Center and a University

The Puerto Rican Research and Resources Center was established and incorporated in 1971. The incorporators were: Blanca Cedeño, Hilda Hidalgo, José Moscoso, Francisco Trilla, and Víctor Rivera. I was the agent, founder, and first executive director of the center. All the incorporating people were friends who had worked with me in other institutions. The Puerto Rican Forum gave the original monies to start the center and obtained a first grant from the Ford Foundation until the center was incorporated. The second grant came directly to the Research and Resources Center.

My intention was to develop an educational institution that would begin with a strong research component, creating the foundation for the first Puerto Rican educational institution of higher education. This was implementing an idea that had been incorporated in the Puerto Rican Community Development Project in 1964. The center opened its doors with two projects. One was to produce a bibliography of books, research studies, art works, periodicals and magazines, audio-visual and recorded materials by and about Puerto Ricans. The second project was to create a program of eight fellowships for Puerto Ricans studying at the master and doctoral levels if they would select a topic of study related to the Puerto Rican population. The center secured contributions for free tuition for the students selected by the center. The tuition scholarships were obtained from the universities where the students had secured entry. The first year, the eight students selected had been admitted to City University, Queens College, School of Social Work, Teachers' College of Columbia University, and George-town University. This program was funded by our basic grant from the Ford Foundation and a grant from the Fund for the Improvement of Post-Secondary Education (FIPSE) of the U.S. Department of Education to add two seminars a year for students to receive extra assistance in completing their theses and dissertations. The seminars were held at the campus of Goddard College in Vermont, and Dr. Peggy Sanday, an anthropologist from Carnegie Mellon University, organized the content and identified other faculty participants for the seminars.

The bibliography was organized by Paquita Vivó, a Puerto Rican woman who lived in Washington, D.C., and was well respected by the press and writers. She was instrumental in introducing me to other Puerto Ricans whom we employed in the Puerto Rican Research and Resources Center. R.R. Bowker, a well-known publisher of source books, published the bibliography.

Very soon after its establishment in 1972, the Research Center purchased a house on Church Street, one of the streets that end in

Dupont Circle. Houses in Washington were easily acquired back then because they were abandoned and their prices were low. The house was restored under my direction, and the Center moved in.

As the Research Center developed its work, we submitted a proposal to conduct a study on the reasons why Puerto Rican students drop out of high school. The U.S. Office of Education Fund for the Improvement of Post-Secondary Education funded the proposal. Dr. Peggy Sanday and Dr. Fred Ericson from Harvard University were part of the group of researchers who worked on the format and questionnaire for the study. A group of Puerto Rican students and parents were involved in helping to develop the questionnaire. The questionnaire was given by trained Puerto Ricans from the areas where the students lived. It was our philosophy and commitment that the study could only be valid if the people who were to be the studied actually participated in the design and implementation of the study. Three communities were included in the study: New York City; Vineland, New Jersey; and Philadelphia, Pennsylvania.

The third project of the center, as described in the proposal funded by the Ford Foundation, was to explore the establishment of a bilingual community college for Puerto Rican students. To realize this objective, I organized a panel of educators who could participate in this process. One of the people I contacted was Professor Hilda Hidalgo, who was on the faculty of Rutgers University in New Jersey. Hilda was a friend as well as a colleague. Hilda accepted and came to Washington, D.C., to meet with the panel of advisors. It is here that my life took an unexpected turn, because Hilda had also come to talk with me about her doctoral work in a very innovative school. Hilda was very excited about her own study and encouraged me to call Dr. Roy Fairfield, one of the founders of the Union Graduate School where she was pursuing her doctoral work. I was not interested in returning to school, as I was deeply immersed in the development of the Research Center. But at her insistence, I called. The call to Dr. Fairfield was a rewarding experience. Roy knew of me and my work and informed me that the Union was seeking creative and productive people who could continue their community work while pursuing a doctoral degree. He visited me in Washington, D.C., and we talked about my application. He also had an opportunity to meet with the master and doctoral students who were working at the center. Roy was impressed by our students and the model of education that we had developed to support the students through their graduate programs while engaging them to work on problems of interest and need for their communities. Roy was also able to experience firsthand the work of a group of staff and consultants who were compiling the annotated bibliography. On staff, he also met our new librarian, Ms. Lourdes Miranda-King, who would become the librarian for Universidad Boricua.

Roy was truly impressed and urged me to complete my application. He offered me assistance in developing the description for my project demonstrating excellence (PDE), which was required for meeting graduating requirements. The Union Graduate School was the doctoral level of the University Without Walls that came about in the 1970s in the United States. In a response to students' protests and faculty demands for innovation and relevance in the programs of traditional universities, twenty-seven universities had joined efforts to establish a new educational process that would return the students to the center of the learning experience. The effect would be to create a new and innovative learning community, breaking down archaic and irrelevant structures and processes. The movement of educational reform would change the way students learned and the way that teachers taught. Union Graduate School was at the forefront of the movement for educational reform.

I completed all my application materials and I was accepted. I became a doctoral student in the summer of 1972. My life as administrator of the Research Center and student in a doctoral program served to integrate my activities for the next three years. During my participation in the program, I accepted the responsibility of assisting in organizing a class on comparative economic systems. Students were encouraged to organize classes in their areas of interest. Two of the faculty who were economists taught the course. The content covered the economic activities of human beings from primitive days to the present. The course traced the processes by which a human group provides for its needs and wants; its development of systems of production, division of labor, distribution; and the responses to the use of accumulated goods and products. It also studied the manner by which the group or its members acquire and use power to control the multiple processes.

I had never been exposed before to this kind of thinking or content. I became an avid reader and continued my reading in the area of economics, far beyond the requirements of the course. I turned my attention and learning to areas relating to the emerging radical analysis of society; the challenges to traditional paradigms; theories of neocolonialism; alternative teaching methodologies; historical presentations on world domination by colonial powers; race and racism; sexual politics; and the role of the United States in the history of Puerto Rico. This was when I fully understood the role of the United States in developing its own political power and resources through the economic and political exploitation of other countries, including my own. I understood the role of agencies such as the FBI and the CIA, controlling movements for change and national liberation in Puerto Rico and other Latin American countries.

I was learning. I was excited and integrating my new learning into my work with my community and in the development of an educational process and model that would address issues of oppression and was designed to empower learners to become agents for social change. At the same time that my work was progressing and I was learning, I was becoming very bitter because I was concluding that the poverty and societal inequities were so entrenched that it would be very difficult to make substantive, permanent changes. I often reminded myself of my earlier interests in the study of social policy formulation and implementation. I was now on the right track for obtaining information that would politicize my thinking and help me find explanations for situations of poverty, who was poor and excluded, and how the processes were sustained. I must confess to you that at this point in my life, I felt despair in believing that any change in these conditions was possible.

I spent days feeling depressed and lost. I would come home early and listen to music or take long walks in the park behind my house. I was now living in a townhouse on Nebraska Avenue. For a few days, I was not thinking. I was in a state of suspension. This was followed by my returning to my roots and reading poetry in Spanish. I reread Julia de Burgos, Alfonsina Storni, Gabriela Mistral, and Juana de Ibarbourou, who were the top women poets of our world to the south. Then I went looking for the works of poets of rebellion, Miguel Hernández of the Spanish Civil War and Pablo Neruda of more recent rebellious communications. These readings helped me to break the period of disconnection, and I began to feel myself connected once more with my world.

The work of the Research and Resource Center continued with the administration and consultation and planning of many panels of educational advisors composed of community people, students, and educators. The research project and the teaching with the research students continued. I was fully immersed in curriculum development, educational models, and structures for the school.

One day I was having my lunch on the grass at Dupont Circle with one of my fellow students from the Union Graduate School when the news came that President Nixon had ordered the arrest of people who were demonstrating in the streets of the capital. After the arrest of the demonstrators, the police swept the streets, arresting citizens whether they were in the demonstrations or not. We ran to the Center to see the news on television. We saw pictures of the police arresting innocent people who were walking on the sidewalks. A stadium was opened to detain those arrested. These activities created a public uproar of protest by various citizens' groups because of the blatant violation of civil rights. Rapidly, the president asked for people to be processed and released from the detention arena. I was personally so outraged that I made a public announcement to my staff that I was going to quit my studies and use the funds to buy guns for the revolutionary efforts in Puerto Rico. I said that I would join these efforts directly instead of studying for a doctorate.

My classmate John became very upset and begged me to reconsider such a drastic decision. He said that he would leave me to think about my decision. A staff member from Puerto Rico, whom they called Bambino, asked me to accompany him on a walk. He said, "Each person has a role in the struggle. I and those younger will go to the front and fire guns. Your role is to teach and inspire us to build institutions, write and guide us with your ideas. You are not going to withdraw from school. We need your knowledge and wisdom." Bambino was about fifteen years younger than I was. He became my teacher. His words shocked me. I have never forgotten him or his words to me.

This conversation and my continuous reflections ended my depression and feelings of not knowing what to do. I remembered that there were groups of committed people with progressive ideas, and our collective work could be a countervailing power to create a more humane and just world. I reminded myself that I was not alone, nor was I unique. There are others who, like me, work at this very hard, but not impossible, quest.

At about the same time that I was coming through my own doubts and finding my way back, a man came to my office to ask me to become a member of a national commission that he was organizing. It was the Study Commission on Undergraduate Education and the Education of Teachers (SCUEET). He informed me that he had secured my name from various sources and that he knew of my interest in improving education. His name was Dr. Paul Olson, a professor of medieval English and poetry at the University of Nebraska. As the head of the commission, he had received several million dollars to organize a panel of sixty exceptional educators who would work together and design a method and process for achieving the reform of postsecondary education and the education of teachers. The commission would include schoolteachers, faculty, activists, scholars, and students. By the end of the interview, we were calling each other Paul and Toni. Paul was an exceptional human being and a unique and dedicated educator. When he came into our offices, several of us had been taken aback by his physical dress and appearance. He wore very old wool pants with high work shoes that were full of mud and clay. His shirt was wool plaid and discolored, with the collar of the jacket half out, no tie, and no overcoat. By the time he left, I knew that I had met an exceptional human being, intelligent, committed, sensitive, sincere, and very concerned with the future of the country and the miseducation of our youth in the universities of the nation. He explained that what I was doing with the Research Center to develop a university was exactly what the nation needed. He offered the commission as the vehicle to achieve my objective. In the commission, I would meet other educators trying to establish universities owned and developed by communities of poor and disenfranchised peoples: Chicanos, Native Americans, Afro-Americans, Appalachians, artists, and farmers. He believed that the commission could demonstrate to the nation how to educate disenfranchised peoples from multiple and diverse backgrounds. He left me a large collection of books and materials to read in preparation for the first meeting. He, in turn, took materials explaining the Puerto Rican Research Center's mission, philosophy, and objectives, along with the model of the educational institution that we proposed to develop.

In the commission, I came into contact with educators in the black community from Chicago: Barbara Sizemore and Bill Smith. I also met and visited with the founders of colleges: D.Q. University, Nairobi College, Aztlán, Malcolm X College, Oglala Sioux Community College, Sinte Gleska College Center, and El Museo del Barrio. All these communities were planning or had already moved to develop their own community-based ethnic colleges. In the first meeting of the commission I met a young Puerto Rican man who was a member of the students' committee of the commission. His name was Angelo Falcón. He had been a student in ASPIRA. We met in Racine, Wisconsin, at the Frank Lloyd Wright house where the commission met. Meeting them, I realized that our dream of having a university was possible. I became the chairperson of the Committee on Cultural Pluralism that worked and produced the commission's official definition for cultural pluralism. The committee produced a book: *Badges and Indication of Slavery: Cultural Pluralism Defined.* James Bowman, Barbara Blourock, and I were the principal editors.

My experience in this commission made it possible for me to develop the comprehensive philosophy for Universidad Boricua, and the work provided me with the motivation and the resources to make the university a reality. During this time, the staff and advisors had made the decision to pursue a university and to amend the bylaws of the corporation to assume the name Universidad Boricua—Puerto Rican Research and Resources Center. It was clear that we were moving in the right direction, and others approved of the change, including the Fund for the Improvement of Post-Secondary Education that was now funding our efforts. We knew that it would take as much effort to complete a university as a community college, and we changed the original name that had been selected, Ramón E. Betances Community College, in favor of the new name, Universidad Boricua. We decided to pursue accreditation for the B.A. degree.

As part of my studies at the Union Graduate School, I had committed myself to a document presenting a total plan, including academic structure, administration, and governance, as well as the fiscal plan, for the university. Through the commission, I learned about the obstacles that had to be overcome in obtaining the license to teach, about the origins of accreditation, the biases of traditional institutions in imposing standards, the nature of "academic turf wars," the separation of knowledge by disciplines, and the role of universities in developing knowledge and sustaining societal power relations. I was gaining a clearer understanding of how our institutions had to be different because we needed to empower our students and provide them with the knowledge and skills to rebuild communities that had been destroyed. I knew that the education in our institution had to be explicitly and purposefully involved in problem-solving processes. It also needed to provide our students with an opportunity for learning in a process that valued them and liberated them to invest in their educational experience. With such an enormous task, I knew that it would not be possible to complete the planning of the university during the time of my doctoral program, but I felt that I could provide a clear methodology and curriculum for teaching, accompanied by a process to secure permission and ultimately obtain accreditation.

The plan included outreach that would locate learning centers in storefronts in Puerto Rican neighborhoods in three cities: New York, Philadelphia, and Chicago or Boston. We held planning meetings with potential students in these cities. We met them in their homes and communities to understand their needs, their limitations for entering school, and their resources for completing a degree.

In hindsight, this effort may sound complicated, but in the early 1970s, there were many sites where community-based learning institutions were in formation. We were all engaged in a truly radical and revolutionary idea. We at Universidad Boricua were part of a new wave of thinking for alternative education.

I enjoyed immensely the planning meetings with the community groups, as well as the work on designing the learning centers. We consulted the Open University in London. We secured different models for learning modules. Finally, we evolved modules for teaching to be used by our learners through television sets located in the learning centers, which would allow each learner to enter and complete courses at his or her own pace. Self-evaluating guides accompanied these. We incorporated the idea of periodic learning committees to balance the individual learning aspects of the process.

Finally, we began the process of recruiting students and securing the financial support of grants and loans. Relationships had been established with other academic institutions of higher education. A small, competent teaching and administrative staff was put in place.

As was my pattern, I worked so hard on the university that my health was again affected. My asthma had become acute. I could not breathe at night, and it interfered with my sleep so that I could not recover my strength for the following day. My doctor in Washington strongly recommended that I move away from the city. He told me that the city was part of a belt of pollution and that I should have never relocated there. He opened a map of the United States and directed me to relocate to one of two areas. One area was Arizona; the other was San Diego. He also gave me the name of an asthma specialist, Dr. David Mathieson, affiliated with Scripps Hospital in San Diego, who was undertaking a pilot study with asthma patients. He wrote a letter of referral to Dr. Mathieson and left me with the decision as to what I would do. I was again very ill, and I felt that I could not continue to threaten my life by ignoring my health.

I informed the board of my plans to leave Universidad Boricua, and we began a process to recruit a new administrative head. The decision for my replacement was thoroughly discussed, and several possibilities were developed, including a sharing of administrative responsibility by persons on staff. The board knew that the institution would need a person with the credentials necessary to carry Universidad Boricua through the credential process and to be credible to current and prospective funders. The board began a search for president. I was part of the search process. I traveled to Stanford University to interview Professor Frank Borilla. The search committee also held meetings with Dr. Luis Nieves Falcón of the University of Puerto Rico. Dr. Isaura Santiago, who had just accepted a position with the Columbia University Teachers' College, was also interviewed. For various reasons, these people could not accept the position. Finally, the board discussed the idea of inviting a faculty member who was teaching at Columbia University but had not completed his doctorate. We consented to the plan for the person to complete the doctorate while serving as president. Víctor Alicea was solicited and accepted the position in 1973. Víctor had been known to board members as a recipient of an ASPIRA scholarship to complete his master's degree in social work. At the time of the appointment, Víctor was teaching at the planning department of Columbia University.

Prior to my leaving and moving, I planned to leave Universidad Boricua in a sound financial condition with capable, experienced administrators who had worked with me for several years. The university was in receipt of the grant from FIPSE, and relationships had been established with other academic institutions of higher education, which offered their accreditation to Universidad Boricua students as they completed their degree programs. These institutions—among them Antioch College, Goddard College, and others—also offered to assist the staff and board of Universidad Boricua in the further development of the institution.

After I left, Víctor Alicea would take the foundation and resources of Universidad Boricua into a solid academic situation, moving the institution from Washington, D.C., to New York City, and receiving accreditation for offering B.A.s and additional degrees. Members from the original board and staff, who had begun the institution with me, stayed on to assist him. Among the original staff were Carlos García, Roberto Aponte, Lourdes Miranda, Orlando Pérez, Julianne Hau, and Annie Ortiz. The building in Washington, D.C., was sold, and Víctor moved Universidad Boricua to New York City. In New York City, the institution secured accreditation and changed its name to Boricua College.

California

Considering the precariousness of my health, I recalled that when I was living in Puerto Rico and doing consulting outside the country, I had visited Joe Aguayo who lived in San Diego. Joe had worked with me in organizing the Puerto Rican Institute for Political Participation. He was completing an internship as a national urban fellow with the mayor of San Diego. On a previous visit, Joe had invited me to his home in San Diego where I met the dean of the School of Social Work at San Diego State University. At the meeting, the dean offered, but I did not accept, a full professorship at the School of Social Work. Although I did not accept the teaching position, I enjoyed the contact with the faculty I met at Joe's house. These persons included Chicano faculty who taught at San Diego State and the University of California, San Diego. I had especially enjoyed a very challenging conversation with Professor Wilhelmina Perry who taught social policy at the School of Social Work. I was impressed with Perry's intelligent ideology and her commitment to minority students. Perry was a black woman married to a Puerto Rican, and had spent all of her married life living in contact with Puerto Rican communities in New York, Philadelphia, and now in San Diego.

Since my memories of San Diego had been so positive, and I had been offered a teaching position some time ago, I thought seriously of moving to San Diego. I wrote to the dean of the School of Social Work, Dr. Kurt Reichert, and he answered positively, setting up an appointment for me to be interviewed by faculty and students. I successfully completed the interviews, and I was offered an associate professorship position, which I accepted. I sold the house in Washington, D.C., and, with my boxes of books, papers, furniture, and my big German shepherd dog, Max, I moved to San Diego. Barbara, who lived with me, came with me, she had been offered a position of student counselor at the university. The dean searched and located a house that I would purchase.

The initial entrance to San Diego was a disaster. My new house was full of fleas, and had a front yard where the grass had not been cut for many months. We did not unpack, but instead looked for another house near the university. In a short time, we moved into a clean and comfortable California ranch-style house.

Living in California has always been an enigma to me. I have a lot to be grateful for about my life in San Diego. I regained my health. I was very successful as a teacher and as an administrator of the undergraduate program at the School of Social Work. I purchased a beautiful house and established a comfortable and attractive home. I developed a very full relationship with another person who matched my capacity to build dreams into a reality. I fully developed my ideological understanding of power, oppression, the roots of poverty, and the colonization of countries and their people.

Living in California, I came into contact with many strong movements and many ideas and attitudes that could not be found in other areas of the country at the time. I am referring, among others, to such philosophical beliefs that humans are the stewards of the land and are responsible for caring for the natural environment. This belief is found in preambles to the state's constitution and is implemented in policies and institutions. Another very impressive belief for me was the care and advocacy for the handicapped and senior citizens. In California, when I lived there, drivers were expected to stop for pedestrians or they would receive a summons. There was also a very strong movement for the pursuit of health, taking care of the body and mind, almost to an exaggerated point of making it a fetish or religious movement. Two of the new habits that I acquired in California were not eating red meat and exercising daily.

With all these good attributes, it was in San Diego where I experienced intimidating parades of young men dressed in black, holding Dobermans and German shepherd dogs. It was also in San Diego where I experienced going into a telephone booth where a luminous sticker would change from the head of a black man into an orangutan. In other telephone booths, you could find stickers saying "Dial a Nazi message." This type of message came to you by telephone, leaflets, and booklets distributed at public events. I felt constantly in danger in ways that I had not experienced in New York. I missed New York.

I should be able to say that I loved San Diego and California, but I did not. I felt displaced in California, away from my home, always waiting to return. However, I did not know for sure where home was.

A Professor Again

I remember very well my initial teaching experience in California. Having read the main text, several articles on the subject, and other books on the topics of the day, I would thoroughly prepare for my class. I thought that I was well prepared to encounter students who, I expected, would also be well prepared. This had been my experience at Columbia University. From the first weeks of teaching, I found that no one in the class had read the assigned readings, and, of course, no one had even noticed that I had included other sources than the text-book. Very soon I realized that I needed to find new approaches to teaching. I divided my course into units so that students needed to use life situations at home, in the neighborhood, on television, in inter-views on campus, or any other life situation of their choice. They entered the learning process with excitement. I remembered that I had learned about teaching-learning as a process initiated by the learner in two experiences at Universidad Boricua and at the Union Graduate School. From then on, my classes became interesting for me and for them. At San Diego State University School of Social Work, students evaluated teachers, and I began to receive high evaluations.

Alongside the relationships with my students were my relation-ships with the faculty. The relationships with the students were new to me. Before, I had not had white, Jewish, Irish students linger after class and come to my office to chat. Here in San Diego, I had many of these, including older women and men who were my students in the evening classes. My relationship with the faculty was different. At first, I was a strange kind of person to my peers. They knew that I had established a university, that I had been a commissioner in a national body to study and change undergraduate education. They also knew about many of my accomplishments. This caused a separation between them and me. I think that they preferred to pretend that they were not aware all I had done. I must say that I never let them forget it, either. I had a closer relationship with the minority faculty, especially with Professor Wil-helmina Perry.

Kurt Reichert, the dean of the school, had assigned Professor

Perry to guide me into the social policy sequence of the school, for which she was the coordinator and in which I would be teaching. Perry and I had more than one connection. She was married to a Puerto Rican and had visited the island many times. The main and most important linkage between us was the fact that she was a New Yorker in the wilderness of San Diego, which became a very strong and important bond. We talked constantly about books, about ideas to change the social policy sequence, about New York, about policy, about the problems of our profession, and particularly about our school of social work and its limitations. I would be in her office several times a day. Soon Barbara Blourock, Wilhelmina Perry, and I were "the trio" from New York to the students and the faculty. One of the immediate results of the close friendship between Mina Perry and me was the change we brought to the curriculum and the faculty of the undergraduate program. First, we changed the philosophy, teaching approach, and readings of the social policy courses. We taught students to analyze the society in which they lived and to identify policies and how these policies affected their lives and the lives of their family, friends, and community.

Up to the time Dr. Perry and I began changing the teaching content of the social policy courses, these were taught as a historical listing of policies and laws passed to create certain programs to serve people. These teachings were evaluated through true-false exams. Dr. Perry and I taught students how to think, how to use the policy formulation processes as change instruments, how people can participate in influencing the decisions of the policymakers, how citizens are engaged in being consumers and buying not what they need but what they are indoctrinated to think that they want and need. Evaluation of what students learned was measured by the presentation of end-of-semester projects and papers, which they could do alone or in a group. These were usually expanded versions of the presentations done in class. There was a lot of discussion of our capacity to think—analyze, synthesize, integrate, remember—and the fact that in order to be responsible citizens and to make decisions that affect our well-being, these functions and capacities of the brain had to be used consciously to affect the kind of world we want to live in. We both taught two policy courses: one on policy formulation and the second on how policies create services and programs. We both wished to make the policy courses the core curriculum offerings for the undergraduate program, teaching the courses as public, social, international, and economic policies of the country. We succeeded in doing it, but when I resigned as head of the undergraduate program and from teaching in the school, all the changes we had instituted went back to the way they had been before we arrived.

We changed the relationship of students and faculty and the participation of students in the governance of the undergraduate program, having students participating in faculty committees and faculty meetings. Because the undergraduate program was larger than the graduate program, the changes also influenced the graduate students. The combined student body called an all-day convocation of faculty and students to evaluate the behavior of the dean. They subsequently sent a communication to the president of the university protesting the objectionable behavior of the dean with faculty and students. The dean was removed.

Many changes happened during the years of our leadership in the school. Mina and I began to attend conferences and present papers before the Council on Social Work Education. Mina made me a member of a commission that she chaired, the Western Interstate Commission on Higher Education (WICHE). We organized a committee on research with minority communities, which published a collection of papers on the subject. I was appointed director of the undergraduate program, and Mina was elected to the university curriculum committee.

There was, however, one obvious lesson we learned. Despite all the changes we made, the university environment resists change. For example, as director of the undergraduate program, I tried to sponsor faculty colloquia on important topics in higher education or on basic philosophical or scientific ideas that affected our teaching. I would ask specific members of the faculty to make presentations at faculty meetings, but the people either would not attend the meetings or would make a superficial presentation not worth listening to. It was impossible to provoke and sustain collegial thinking and teaching. This was a body of people invested in "Who has an office with a window or a larger one than mine," "I want the courses that meet during midday and early afternoon, so I do not have to come into school early or come in at night," "Who is sleeping with whom?" "Who will get tenure this year or will receive an increase in salary?" and other questions of that kind. Wilhelmina Perry and I, with our undergraduate students' leadership, created an oasis of learning that produced an excitement of discovery and creation that the young can find in productive engagement. Soon these relationships began to bear fruit. At meetings in my house, Barbara, Wilhelmina, a group of graduate and undergraduate students, a few other faculty members, and I discussed ideas for the format, knowledge, content, methods of learning, central philosophy, and ultimate goals for a different kind of university. While this group met during evenings and on weekends, other important events were occurring at the School of Social Work.

The process of selecting a new dean was the most important one happening at the school. The search reached out through the entire country to social work faculty and administrators. Mina, Barbara, and I were acting as watchdogs, bringing the names of blacks, Puerto Ricans, Chicanos, Jews, and women who were good scholars and good administrators, but we were also vigilant as to their commitment to inclusion of minorities in the student body, the faculty, and the knowledge content. From application letters, curriculum vitae, and lists of potential candidates, different people were invited to visit the school for interviews with groups of faculty, students, community leaders, and members of the school leadership. After a long search and many interviews, a relatively young social worker from Pennsylvania was chosen. He appeared to have a very interesting background and showed in his writings and in the interviews a solid philosophical concern with ethical values, commitment to change, and the pursuit of a knowledge base for the profession of social work. But soon it became clear to us that our mission, our sense of leadership, and our use of authority were opposite to his. He believed in an authoritarian form of governance, and it became increasingly difficult for me and other faculty to tolerate his leadership style. Faculty relationships deteriorated and fear and suspicion became central to how we dealt with one another.

I resigned from the school in the fall of 1977. I made the decision that tenure, even early tenure, and position were not more important than my self-respect. I also resigned for health reasons. I had developed a chronic knee condition that, treated improperly, immobilized the knee, making it necessary for me to use a wheelchair and crutches.

We Teach Community Development

While we were all employed by the university, Mina, Barbara, and I were organizing the Graduate School for Urban Resources and Social Policy. We received a grant from the National Endowment for the Arts for developing the component of the school called the Multicultural Art Institute. I was elected by our board of trustees as the president of the school. Our trustees were representatives from the humanities, fields of education, administration, business, community, social work, community development, and social policy. The trustees grew in number as we enrolled students from other communities throughout the country. The graduate school was organized as an alternative institution of higher education that was unique, although it incorporated some features of the Union Graduate School where I obtained my Ph.D., and some of the features of the university I founded in Washington, D.C. Our graduate school in San Diego had a solid philosophical and theoretical base. In addition to the Multicultural Art Institute, it had an Institute for Social Development, an Institute for the Study of Values, and a Community Development Institute.

We established the school in a building in downtown San Diego. Mina and I had developed a knowledge of real estate, and this culminated in our buying several properties in the city. We began this activity because we became aware that resigning tenured positions in a state university had made us economically vulnerable. We had no income, no medical plan, and no pension until our school would be able to employ us. Trying to find a way of developing a retirement plan that would complement our Social Security pension, we began to study the economy of San Diego, searching for an economic activity for two social workers to earn some money and create wealth. We soon found out that in San Diego, real estate was the money-making business. San Diego had an underdeveloped downtown area that had suffered years of neglect because the navy occupied the best real estate in town and created a zone of prostitution, tattoo, and porno shops that blighted the waterfront and the old historic city. I found myself bringing out old Jane Jacobs books about how we have destroyed cities in this country and what makes a healthy city. Mina and I would comb the downtown, identifying the good buildings and good real estate possibilities. We read all about buying property. We found that the process of investing in real estate started with buying a potentially good income property, selling it, buying another, a more expensive one, and repeating this until one found a good building that would bring a large income. We did just that: first we bought a small complex of apartments that we fixed up and sold, making a profit. From this first purchase, we found a very good two-story corner building in the historic downtown area.

During that time, an ambitious politician who was the county chairperson on his way up to becoming a congressman, approached me. He wanted me to help him make a name with an issue that would take him far, so he latched onto a movement that was being discussed in magazines and daily papers. It was called integrated planning. I had a package of materials that I collected from a conference in Washington, D.C., on integrated planning. A student of one of our social policy classes, who was hired by our aspiring politician, brought the ideas on integrated planning to this county chairperson, who immediately named a committee for integrated planning and asked me to be a member of it. The committee published its plans that showed the navy would be moving from the choice spots on the waterfront. There would be money for a massive redevelopment of the old historic buildings in the area, and a comprehensive plan was developed and accepted by the city. A full development plan was designed for the coming changes and placed on exhibit. Dr. Perry and I made the decision to sell our investment property and buy property downtown. We bought a building one block from a planned shopping plaza where the best stores in the west would be built, but where, at the time, drunks, prostitutes, and sailors were hanging around all day and night.

This is the area where we established the Graduate School for Urban Resources and Social Policy. In a way, it was a very significant place to start our work. The graduate school was given permission to teach by the California Department of Education, and we began to enroll students immediately. We wanted to teach people from communities of color who wanted to address problems in their communities that caused harm to their people. They would come to the graduate school to find solutions to problems through research and social and economic policy. We required that the student be sponsored by an institution in his or her community who could benefit from the results of the student's work.

The model of learning in the graduate school was based on a philosophy, a theoretical and conceptual base about the human community that I will summarize here. We believed that human beings invent community because, without it, they cannot survive, grow, and develop to their full potential. People invent community because they need it. If any aspect of community becomes dysfunctional or is destroyed, people can reinvent it. We knew from our own education in sociology and anthropology that communities develop institutions to fulfill the needs of their members. We also knew that the community institutions were organized into systems that perform functions essential for the health and well-being of the members of the community. We also knew that when one of the systems malfunctions, social problems are created.

The learning process in the graduate school was divided into three processes. During the first process, students went through experiences that helped them realize that to learn means to be able to exercise the capacity to think: analyzing, synthesizing, and integrating facts, information, and knowledge. They learned that they were capable of using their intellectual capacities to study their community and identify the functions and institutions that had been destroyed or damaged. More importantly, they also learned that they and their community could reinvent or repair the destroyed function. The most important realization that they obtained from this method of problem identification and problem solving was that it is not the people of the community who are sick or responsible for the existence of social problems. They also would discover the forces in the overall society that are responsible for the destruction of functions and institutions in their community. The plan of work to rebuild the community and its institutions and functions must design steps to aid in the recovery of the community, attacking the true sources of the problem. The students also learned that to design a plan to resolve the problem, their community needs to accrue power, since power is the essential element in the successful creation of change. Power was studied in all its dimensions.

After this very basic and initial presentation of the approach and method of work in the graduate school, the students began their plan of work to use the knowledge acquired in achieving social change—change of a problem in their own community. At this point, they would leave the first phase of their studies in the graduate school facilities.

The model of education was conceptualized and organized so that the learner could complete a major part of the work in his or her community. Following the first California-based seminar, learners returned to their homes to work on an independent educational plan, using a research faculty member from the graduate school. These were research faculty affiliated with various universities in Puerto Rico and the United States who elected to teach with the graduate school because of their own professional and personal commitments to furthering the goals of community empowerment and community restoration in Third World communities. They were able to work part-time with us while continuing in their full-time positions. Our students were from various locations: northern and southern California, Texas, Arizona, the Northeast (New York, New Jersey, Washington, D.C.), and San Diego. The ethnic population of the students was as diverse as their home locations. They were Native Americans from several Native American nations, Chinese, Filipinos, black Americans, Chicanos and Mexican Americans, Vietnamese, Puerto Ricans, and white Americans.

The experience of working outside of our communities was entirely new for all of us. We had to broaden our frame of analysis, values, and working strategies to embrace others who had been victimized and/or excluded from the opportunities of the society. We were now teaching others who shared varying degrees of exclusion, but who also were unable to envision or act upon the knowledge that they had a rightful place within a society that promised opportunities. We were thinking through and clarifying our own ideas in the process and finding ways to have people understand the varying degrees of oppression and denial of rights. Our ideas appeared in an article Mina and I wrote, "Cultural Pluralism: A Goal to be Realized," in *Voices from the Battlefront: Achieving Cultural Equity.*

The graduate school was one of several institutions involved in community-based education. We were members of the Clearing House for Community-Based Free-Standing Education Institutions headquartered in Washington, D.C. In the association's publication "Community Home: Community-Based Education and the Development of Communities" (1979), Mina Perry and I presented one of the papers, "The University: An Institution for Community Development," in which we discussed the history, mission, and origins of the movement for community-based education:

> Community-based alternative education became an appropriate strategy for recreating and creating new institutions that would address these multiple (social) problems. The mission of the new community-based institution included the commitment to social change and community service through scholarship and the opening of access opportunities for previously excluded student populations . . . . If the goal is community development, the educational process must build in the values, standards, and accountability process that challenge learners to make commitments to their communities of origin or preference and to bring substantive knowledge that can be used in the development of the members of the community . . . . Community-based institutions must involve themselves in a continuous analysis of society, and the action/research strategies that can facilitate empowerment for all segments of the society. We are attempting to involve learners, community persons and policymakers in a series of learning/teaching strategies that respond to a comprehensive and holistic analysis of community development as an institutional mission. (28–32)

The association, unlike the commission where I previously had worked, had a distinct and explicitly articulated mission of community development/restoration for its members.

We continued our work of refining our curriculum and defining and implementing the administrative structure to receive our first visit from the California State Department of Education. In spite of our apprehensions, the experience was a rewarding one. The panel arrived at the graduate school, and their initial reactions were of reservation, curiosity, and the questioning of our innovative approach to education. Fully prepared, we presented our educational philosophy, the rationale for the educational model, the curriculum content, and methodology. We had to present and justify the rationale for organizing a curriculum for a newly developing field of study, community development. We also had to present and explain the rationale for our six content areas: theories of community and community development, theories of change, logic and communication, comparative philosophical beliefs, esthetics, ethics, and research methodologies. Since Dr. Perry and I had extensive teaching background in community development and social policy, as well as administrative background and curriculum development experience from having taught in traditional educational institutions, we were clear, confident, and knowledgeable in our presentation. We had researched, studied, and analyzed all new programs in the field of community development. At this time, very few existed. The proliferation of programs in the field would appear during years following our opening. Based on our analysis, we had determined that the basic flaws in the traditional curriculum had to do with the failure to select and organize content that provided learners with theoretical foundations, skills, and philosophical and practical approaches for problem solving in their communities.

When the visiting committee left, they congratulated us. Several of the members offered us help in the next stage in the process of accreditation. Some members asked to come back and visit to see the work of the students. We were elated and felt we could be successful in obtaining full accreditation. We continued with our teaching and our processes toward accreditation although we were mindful of the increasing pressures that the accrediting process imposed upon us. The preoccupation to meet the state standards forced us to conform to standards that were more traditional than we wanted. Into our third year, a small group of students began to confront us, requesting that we award them a degree lowering the criteria we had established. They complained that if ours was a minority institution, why should we demand as much as other institutions? They prepared a document requesting a meeting to confront us so that we would lower the requirements. It was my opinion that these students were not advocates for their communities; their effort was directed at securing benefits for which they were not willing to work. Their attempts at forcing the graduate school to offer degrees without requiring too much of the minority students made us feel that we had to change our recruitment efforts to reach persons who wished to learn. We also wanted to preserve our own mission and values as an alternative educational community-based institution. After long hours of discussion with the trustees, researchers, faculty, and students, we decided not to pursue accreditation! I remember sitting on a bench in the new park on the bay crying. I looked up and saw Mina crying, too. Mina and I had a few painful weeks because we had aspired to offer members of our communities an avenue to obtain doctoral degrees, because we knew from personal experience how hard the traditional institutions made the road for our people to obtain these titles and awards.

After we recovered from the blow of having given up one of our dreams, we called faculty members to consultation meetings to make some changes for the future of the school. These meetings confirmed our decision to change the name of the school to the Graduate School for Community Development. We had realized that we had many students coming from rural communities. The name "Urban Resources" excluded them. The other big change we needed to make had to do with a very important question: Why should students come to study with us? Will they come to learn, even though there is no degree awarded at the end of the work? The central objective for both Mina and me was to be successful in providing the opportunity for minority and poor young people to see how and why our communities were oppressed, excluded, and outside of access to the opportunities that could help them help themselves. We believed firmly that a leadership that was capable of understanding the process of oppression could emerge. It could lead the community to stand up and fight the forces of oppression. However, we knew that such a leadership had to grow in the values of ethical commitment to their communities and not give in to the temptations and offerings of individual wealth and glory.

We decided to continue with our alternative model and not to change or reduce requirements or expectations. We confirmed our decision to recruit minority leaders but we would recruit directly through community organizations. The organizations would become a vital and significant partner in the learning process with the learner and with the graduate school. The learner was now expected to engage honestly and thoroughly because the organization needed their skills and education to improve and advance the functioning of the agencies.

We went after this population. The question was, could they come? The other population of learners, we decided, could be students who were in traditional institutions of higher education who found they needed help in completing their dissertations. The graduate school would offer help through one of its research faculty if the dissertation addressed a problem the student's community suffered and if the student was ready to engage community people through a committee that would use the dissertation in an effort to address the problem. The learner was required to pay a fee for the work of the research faculty.

We had a few such students come to us for help. But most of the new students came from community agencies in search of knowledge and skills they recognized they did not have. The important thing for the graduate school faculty and trustees was that these learners were engaged in social change efforts. When the new type of students finally came, we were again excited with our school. Students came with projects they were already working on in hopes we would connect them to existing opportunities. Our students would be engaged in legislative confrontations, in serving as aides to politicians who were interested in passing laws on specific problems, in organizing art exhibits, in starting a newspaper in their community, and in other projects. The gathering of data for their research projects was done through traditional research methods, but also through photography, taped interviews, and other nontraditional methods. Because our students were in most cases very poor, the graduate school raised funds for their projects. For example, grants were secured for a project in which Chicano dancers studied the origins of their dances in Aztec culture and for a Chicano mother tracing in county records the school construction contracts of companies that did not hire minority workers. Several students became employees in a project to test the idea of engaging high school students in developing small businesses. The project, funded by the Department of Labor, would demonstrate that the business experience would result in raising the students' grades, helping them to stay in school and graduate. (The projects produced five small businesses, and each of the students stayed in high school and graduated.) The graduate school also secured funds to establish a photography lab, a silk-screening workshop, and a program to place artists, poets, and dancers in elementary schools. An annual arts street festival was instituted to bring the work of artists of diverse racial and cultural communities to the larger San Diego population. During the festival, a juried art exhibition was held to bring to the public the work of unknown painters, sculptors, and photographers. Many of the artists who won the three prizes and mentions of honor were later exhibited in other galleries. We also offered classes to artists on economic development so they would learn how their art could bring economic rewards and, at the same time, teach art appreciation to uninitiated persons. Classes were also offered to community minority persons on the use of art in decorating their homes and in the giving of gifts.

Our Multicultural Art Institute changed the art scene in San Diego, not only in the graphic arts but also in theater. Through projects for which the Graduate School for Community Development obtained grants, a group of performers and dancers came to study in the graduate school. A black theater group performed in our small all-purpose gallery-theater-conference-room facility. They later performed at universities in the area. There is one person who today is a well-known actor who came out of this group—James Avery, who plays the father in the television series *Fresh Prince of Bel Air*. A second theater group that used our facilities was a women's theatrical group, Sisters on Stage, who wrote and performed their own works. Their work usually addressed current problems, such as smoking and the health problems created by it, or the right of women to control their bodies in the reproductive process, or the effect of drinking alcoholic beverages. In this group, another Hollywood and Broadway actress emerged, Kathy Nemgemi, who played one of the nuns in the movie *Sister Act.*

The Graduate School for Community Development was a reality that sustained my interests and those of Mina for twelve years. In 1982, I retired from the presidency of the school and was elected chairperson of the board of trustees. Mina became the president of the school. In May 1982, I received a grant from the U.S. Department of Education's Mina Shaughnessy Scholars Program. This award allowed me to retire from a paid position at the graduate school. The purpose and expected product of the grant was for me to write a book. The theme of the book was "Toward the Development of a Theory of Community Development: The Process of Colonizing and Destroying a Community and the Process of Decolonizing or Redeveloping a Community." These Mina Shaughnessy Awards were given to people who had spent their lives teaching and acting in and about community, and using innovative teaching methods. I developed the book, but was not able to take it through the editing and reediting process to publication. The amount of the grant did not cover the costs of paying an editor and an agent to help secure a publisher. I still have six chapters of the book in my files.

At the age of sixty-one, while I was writing this book, I was invited to attend a conference that the independence forces of Puerto Rico were celebrating in Mexico City. I accepted when I was informed that Puerto Ricans in New York and other states were to have full representation. I also learned that people from the United States who were supportive of liberation movements would be there in solidarity with the people of Puerto Rico who were fighting for the independence of their country. Attendees paid their own expenses and made their own arrangements. I had a terrible fight with the organizers in California because I was listed as "a person in solidarity" with Puerto Rican independence. I "blew my top" when the organizers refused to list me with the Puerto Ricans. I had to call New York City and the contingent traveling from there, so that they would include my name in their list. When they did so, I asked the California group to delete my name from those "in solidarity." They did not want to do this because it would diminish their numbers. I had to tell them in angry tones that I was not in solidarity—"I was it." They were in solidarity with me. I left on my own and joined the New Yorkers after I arrived in Mexico. The president of Mexico sponsored the conference. He covered all expenses for us in Mexico at the Hotel El Presidente. Before the conference opened, we were informed that the American ambassador had visited the president of Mexico to request that the conference be canceled. We were told that, in a very tense meeting, the president of Mexico told the American ambassador that he invited and held conferences in his country with whomever he wanted. The Mexican president said the conference would take place, and he would call the president of the United States to find out if he had requested that the conference be closed. The matter was resolved then, and the conference opened with a welcome and greeting from the Mexican president.

The conference was a wonderful experience. The entire world was in Mexico in solidarity with the independence of Puerto Rico! At the central table were seated Lolita Lebrón, Rafael Cancel Miranda, Irving Flores, and Andrés Figueroa Cordero, the *independistas* who had been in jail for firing on Congress in 1954. Arafat placed shawls on their shoulders and promised that the rest of their presents would be weapons whenever they would need them. One morning, after having breakfast with a group of us from New York, Panamanian university students, faculty members, and labor union leaders presented to the presidential table a symbolic representation of arms, money, and soldiers to fight with us when we called them into our struggle. We received these kinds of offerings from Irish, Nicaraguans, Cubans, Cypriots, and many other fighters for national liberation. Fortunately, when Tomás Borges, the general of the Nicaraguan Revolution spoke, he stated it is not so easy to start a revolution in the situation in which Puerto Rico finds itself. He said the offers of help would be there when it was possible for us to use it. After his statement, I felt better. I had been feeling ashamed that all that help was offered, but we Puerto Ricans were not doing anything to use it.

At the end of the conference, when the organizers were ready to write the final resolution, the Puerto Rican delegation from the United States noticed that the representatives from the island were red-eyed and tired, saying that they had been up all night fighting over the resolution. We Puerto Ricans from the United States were not included in this work, but we inquired why they were fighting. One person said the fight was with the Russian delegate. After we pushed hard, we were informed that the Russian wanted the resolution to list all the struggles around the world and how they were helped by the Soviet Union. At the very end, then, a small description about the struggle in Puerto Rico would be included, listing the countries present. We then agreed that the end content, very much expanded, should begin the resolution with a solemn commitment of support from those present and signing it. Then, at the end, it would recount whatever the Soviets wanted to claim as their help to other countries. Puerto Ricans from the island thought we could not offend the Russians. We from New York said, "We are not going to struggle to get the United States out of being our oppressor to accept the Soviets as our new oppressor. We will not accept them telling us what to do." From our group we elected one person, María Gutiérrez, to go with the island committee to see the Russian. María took the lead in addressing the Russian and in no uncertain terms told him that the resolution as approved by us would be the version used. She told him his suggested format was not approved by us, and, because the conference was about us, our will would prevail.

Before the final session, we were called out in front of the hotel to receive the salute of Mexico City's labor unions marching in solidarity with the independence of Puerto Rico. Almost a thousand workers with the banner of their union, dressed in black with red scarves and caps, with their fists closed and their arms up in salute to us, marched in front of the hotel. They stopped in front of us as they marched and chanted "Viva Puerto Rico libre." We all became emotional and cried. María Canino, María Gutiérrez, and I ran down to join the marchers. We marched for many blocks and spoke with the workers. That was a day I will never forget!

Some months after this solidarity conference, I was invited to attend a conference in Nicaragua on popular education. A group of educators from South, Central, and North America went to Nicaragua in August 1983, to participate in presenting papers and to visit projects in urban and rural areas of Nicaragua. We visited many towns and rural areas to see the educational, artistic, economic, and scientific experiences the people were going through and were conducting. I was so inspired by what I saw and heard that I almost decided to stay and participate in the experiment the Sandinistas were conducting. There were other people from several areas of the world helping with the transformation of the country and its people. Young men and women, students from Germany, Holland, France, Spain, Ireland, the United States, and various countries in the Spanish-speaking world were working side-by-side with Nicaraguans in rebuilding their country. These young students were called *internacionalistas*. A group of scientists from Cuba was teaching Nicaraguan scientists how to mount and operate equipment to convert the leftovers of the sugarcane process into electricity. The equipment had been donated by France, and the Cubans were donating their knowledge and work to set up the machinery. We visited a group of families at work building their houses. These were families that had voluntarily agreed to give up their houses in an area that was going to be flooded to form a lake and a dam that would generate electricity. The families went through months of learning and discussing why they should give up their houses to the government so that the area could be made into a lake. They agreed after months of learning how the lake would be made and how electricity would be produced. They requested that their new houses be constructed in the same order of location as their old houses, so they could live next to their neighbors and maintain their sense of community. They were then trained in construction, and they rebuilt a community shaped in the image of the one they had given up.

Another impressive visit was to a cooperative farm operated fully by the owners of the land before the revolution. Now they operated the food business on it. Most of the farmers were almost illiterate, but with their rudimentary reading and arithmetic skills, they ran the farm as a successful business. One of the farmers, who was the supervisor of the workers and the production process, explained with great pride how the large farm was taken over by the Sandinista government and had been divided into smaller farms given to the families who worked them. The families owned the land as long as they used it to grow food. The land would revert to the government if the owner would not work it for production. After we had seen many farmers at work, women and men, we went to the central office, a crudely built structure with several tables and chairs made by the farmers. At one table we met the bookkeeper who showed us the books, explaining how many oranges, potatoes, bananas, and other produce had been harvested and how much income these brought. The books were kept by hand, but clearly, in a very simple and basic manner. All the workers had learned to read, write, and do basic arithmetic through a massive effort conducted by the Sandinistas after ending the revolutionary war by using the army to teach literacy throughout the entire country. This literacy effort had two objectives: to debrief the soldiers from the horrors of the experience of war, and to attempt to teach the entire nation to read. The educators we spoke to told us both objectives were accomplished.

We saw other impressive programs, such as theater groups traveling all over the country presenting small plays that the audience finished with different endings, according to their understanding of the problem presented. The plays presented were based on unresolved issues and problems the country faced after the revolution. The theater was a tool for teaching.

We also visited villages where there had been attacks by the contras—the guerrillas who were hiding in the jungles and who wished to take the country back from the Sandinistas. This was the group that the United States was supporting. The village people showed us their guns and told us about their daily practices to defend their homes, animals, crops, machinery, and tools. These villagers told us how the contras had come to line them up in the plaza while all the women and children cried. The contra men were crude and vulgar, using abusive language. The women told of the selection of one man from the circle, how his arms had been chopped off in front of everyone, and he was left bleeding on the ground. The villagers reported that everyone was terrified. The contras took the women and raped them in front of everyone. The troops then left the village in flames. After this, the people told us that they feared sleeping at night, terrified that the contras would return. The Sandinista forces had been unable to find the troops in the woods.

The people showed us their wounds, and we could feel the terror of the women whom they had raped. The village people had developed a watch system, training women, men, and children how to use their ammunition and guns. We left the visit full of anguish and anger.

Before we left Nicaragua, we had the unique opportunity of meeting Tomás Borges, who, at the age of twenty-five, was the oldest military leader of the Sandinista army. He told of moving constantly from place to place to avoid being caught because the contras had sworn to kill him. It took three days for this visit to take place. We were kept on alert to stop all activity if the message came that the visit was set. Finally one day, we were picked up by a bus and taken to a meeting place. The meeting place turned out to be in the backyard of a church. Tomás was then a well-built, dark, small man who looked much older than his twenty-five years. He was direct and frank with us in his perception of the length of time that the revolutionary spirit would survive and when their dream of a new political relationship for the country would become a reality. He believed that the United States would not allow Nicaragua to survive. At one point, he asked: "Where is the Puerto Rican?" I identified myself. He continued: "I know what your country has gone through. Those of you who moved to live in the colonial power are suffering still worse. Consider us Nicaraguans a sisterly nation. Take my love." We embraced, and I sat by, openly crying.

We visited a rural village where we observed the teaching methodology that had been so successful in reducing the nation's illiteracy. Books and pencils were scarce. Teachers had prepared teaching books by cutting and pasting photographs and words from old newspapers and magazines. Dried tree twigs were used to write in the sand or the earth. I was so impressed that I wanted to stay and help with the heroic effort.

When I returned home, I told Mina how I wished that I could have remained in Nicaragua. This experience made me feel that I had unfinished work to complete in my own country, Puerto Rico. From that moment on, we talked of how to leave the graduate school in the hands of workers and students who would continue the work. The workers and students were afraid of the ideas. However, one group of artists continued with the work of the Multicultural Arts Institute.

Our plan to move from San Diego was seriously considered by us. We thought that we could do in Puerto Rico the type of work that I had seen in Nicaragua. The move was fully planned. We made trips to the island and selected a house in the village of Cubuy, where we could live, work, and retire.

Seventh Part

I Return to Puerto Rico to Retire
(1984–1998)

Living in the Rain Forest

I planned to return to Puerto Rico and contribute my experience and my knowledge to help the country with its problems. I had dreamed of a semiretirement in which I could work, using the institution we had incorporated in California, the Graduate School for Community Development. I contacted ASPIRA of Puerto Rico, and jointly we held poetry readings and art gallery exhibits. Engaging the interest of a poet friend I knew from New York, Carmen Puigdollers, we started afternoon poetry readings on weekends at ASPIRA. In search of a more permanent type of art project, I thought of the idea of inviting the National Endowment for the Arts (NEA) to give a grant to the city of Carolina for developing a comprehensive art program that would be part of Carolina's redevelopment plans. The mayor of Carolina had been a schoolteacher, and his ideas for the development of Carolina, a town that had been overshadowed by San Juan, included the full use of art to attract artists to live in the town and to encourage the inclusion of all the arts in the curriculum of the schools. We wrote a proposal letter inviting the NEA to consider giving Carolina a challenge grant to develop a comprehensive plan for the inclusion of art in the city development plan. A representative from NEA came to meet with the mayor and his development staff. All the art plans were presented, including the establishment of a fine arts school with music and visual arts. The center of the plan presented to the NEA was the redesigning of the central plaza of the town and the restoration of a historic building on one side of the plaza to become an artists' incubator. The plaza had been modernized into a grotesque center, including a very large, shell-like stage where bands would play. Trees had been removed, and the result was a dismal, ugly disaster that no one used. The historic building had two stories with a large colonial-style balcony.

The representative from the NEA was very pleased and waited for the proposal to be submitted. The mayor promised to invest $150,000 to acquire the building in front of the plaza and restore it with the assistance of the NEA's matching grant. This never happened because the person in the mayor's office assigned to work on it never came through.

Mina and I had decided we were not going to be swallowed by this project unless there was action from the citizens of Carolina. I had learned one thing in all the years of institution building: If the people who will benefit from the institution do not participate in the work needed to establish the institution, they will never act as if the institution belongs to them. They will expect you to administer it for them. We did not want this to happen in Carolina.

We continued to work with ASPIRA of Puerto Rico. The executive director of ASPIRA offered us an office to work in while we awaited our furnishings in transit from San Diego. We occupied this office and worked with a committee of educators who were helping ASPIRA establish a college.

One day, after about two months on the island, a call to Navieras de Puerto Rico, the government freight company, brought the desired and awaited answer that the container with our belongings had arrived. We drove down to the piers of Navieras to see if we could get our furnishings that day since it was early in the morning. We found the container with our belongings was in, but a very officious man refused to accept the fact that inside the container was our Volkswagen. He insisted, repeating it over and over again, that a vehicle could not be inside the container because sending vehicles with the rest of the furnishings was prohibited. I asked him to open the container, but he said the padlock would remain closed until he found out how this had happened. The morning went by. After we ate lunch and returned, we found that the man who was the supervisor still maintained his position. We had been paying for a rented car for about two months and that was eating into our funds very fast, so we needed our vehicle. We said so with anger. A man who did not work for Navieras, but seemed to be a very alert person, said he was going to resolve the matter. He asked for a crowbar and forced the padlock open, showing the Volkswagen inside the container. The supervisor became infuriated, but our rescuer did not pay any attention and brought the container to an area of the pier where the Volkswagen was unloaded. We had the key to it and our legal ownership papers for it. He told us where to take it to be processed. He said he would deal with the man in charge. Nothing would happen to him because he did not work at the piers.

That is the story of how we recovered our belongings. It should have told us how the rest of our time in the country would be spent. That day, I had a premonition that our life on the island would be full of these kinds of experiences.

We bought a house in the rain forest, which we had seen and fallen in love with on a previous trip to the island. It needed a lot of work because it had been vandalized, and all appliances, doors, windows, electrical outlets, shelves, and anything that could be removed, had been stolen. The house had been unoccupied for many years, so it had snakes, rats, and weeds growing in it. We bought it because the architecture was attractive, with beams across the living room ceiling. It was built with a long structure, with the kitchen and one bathroom on one side, the living room-dining room in the middle, and the bedrooms and another bathroom on the other side. The sun streamed in on both sides of the ceiling. There was no other house like this one in the village. It also had an artesian well and a creek that went by the side of the house and ended in the river. The house was constructed on a farm, eighteen acres in size. One side of the property was the river, which contained rocks with petroglyphs made by the Taínos, the original inhabitants of Puerto Rico. Over all, the property was very attractive.

I was so excited about living in the mountains where our aborigines, the Taínos, thought the god of good, Yukiyú, and the god of evil, Huracán, lived. El Yunque, the name of the mountains and of the rain forest, had always had a place in my childhood dreams. When I was a student at the University of Puerto Rico, my family secured an apartment in a new housing project called Las Casas. From the window of my bedroom, I could see the silhouette of the three peaks of El Yunque. I used to sit on the windowsill and draw the peaks, while my brother and sister played around me and marveled at my artwork. I had always wanted to live in El Yunque, where the Taíno gods lived. My brother and sisters, especially the younger one, Haydée, were very impressed by my drawings and stories about the Taíno gods living in El Yunque. The three peaks were always engulfed in heavy, dark clouds. Only on very sunny days would the clouds lift toward midday. It was very understandable that the Taínos thought these peaks were the house of the gods of good and evil.

Having come back to live in Cubuy, this village where the Taínos lived and dealt with their gods, was delightful for me. The name Cubuy means "mountain of water" in the Taíno language. I wanted to find the Taínos in the inhabitants of the village.

We sent money and a design to a friend of ours, Antonio Díaz Royo, and his wife, Cruzma Nazario, who promised to secure a worker and prepare the house for our arrival. But when we arrived, the house was not ready. We found out that workers were very unreliable unless one was present while they worked. We had to occupy the house as it was. Our friends provided us with a borrowed chair-bed, flashlights, bed covers, pillows, and blankets. Cubuy was very cold at night. We had brought inflatable beds, but by the end of the night, the air would escape from the mattresses. We took turns sleeping on the chair-bed. It took several months before our life had the minimal comforts we were used to.

I still intuited that life on the island was going to be a disaster, but I said to myself, *You have to give it a real chance to be fair.* We stopped offering ASPIRA help in organizing the college because life demanded that we organize ourselves at home. We concentrated on making our house in the country livable. Something very interesting happened while doing this. A young man named John Luis (a name we would not expect in the hills of Puerto Rico) came to take a job with us doing general work on the house and the land around the house. The grass was so high you could not see a person walking through it. To cut the grass, the people in the country used a machete. John Luis suggested that we also hire his cousin in order to speed up the cutting, and we agreed. By that time, we had done most of the work on the house and patio. John Luis's young family members became our friends, and we would spend Saturday mornings talking and visiting. From these visits, I learned that these young Puerto Rican men and women, ranging from the ages of fourteen to twenty-one, had lived in the United States, but did not know where San Juan was. These young people did not know the name or number of the road that went down the mountain to join the main thoroughfare that went to San Juan or west to Fajardo. They simply knew that there was a main road, "la carretera principal," as they called it, and they knew the secondary roads went to their home. No road had a name. They knew that "la carretera principal" went to the airport, because they had taken it. They had gone to the Bronx, in New York, to live with relatives and to work—this was the origin of the name "John Luis." Talking more in detail about New York, I found out that to them, anywhere in that city was the Bronx. I discussed with Mina the fact that our young neighbors had no sense of themselves in the world.

These Saturday visits soon became teaching sessions with the help of a map of Puerto Rico, a globe of the world, and one of the chalkboards we brought from San Diego. We tried to teach our young friends where they existed in this world and in their country. I cannot tell if they learned, but we learned that the place called the Bronx in John Luis's mind, where he went to work and live with his uncle, was really Vineland, New Jersey.

Before continuing any further with these Saturday sessions and where they took us, I should mention the impact of our arrival in Cubuy. When our belongings arrived at the pier in San Juan, Navieras de Puerto Rico had to deliver them to our house in Cubuy, as contracted. So the big container with the name Navieras de Puerto Rico came through Road Number 3 from San Juan to Canóvanas, turned right on Road 185, a smaller road that connects Canóvanas with Juncos, and then turned left on a narrower, curvy Road 186 that climbs toward the rain forest. It is one thing to travel on Road 186 in an automobile (which is hard enough for the uninitiated), and another thing for a truck pulling a large van to climb Road 186, with its more than one hundred curves, the mountain on one side, and the drop at the left on the other side. If you happen to allow yourself to look down on your left, you give yourself the fright of your life when you see the distance to the bottom. I, who had learned to drive in California, with its large freeways, learned to drive up and down to Cubuy on Road 186 with great trepidation and fear. The driver from Navieras drove up slowly, cursing all the way. When he and his container arrived at kilometer 7, where he had to turn left to reach our house, he stopped, got out, telephoned his boss and then our house, to say he was not moving any further, and we had to resolve the problem of transporting the furnishings to our door. By the time he telephoned us, we had been told of the problem by many residents who came to our door. We left the house in our Volkswagen to meet the Navieras truck and solve the problem, which was simply that the big Navieras truck could not go up the very narrow road that led to our house.

By the time we arrived at the place where the Navieras truck had stopped, almost all of the inhabitants of the village were around the container, talking, asking questions, and giving opinions as to how to solve the problem. I heard them saying that two "Americans" had come from California to live in the house of the commander of the navy. Our house was called the commander of the navy's house because that was who had originally built and owned it. I called a small moving company recommended by the owner of the local gasoline station. The moving company sent two smaller trucks to transport our furnishings up the hill to our house. The smaller trucks came, and the men who had been standing around helped unload the furniture, boxes of books, and clothing to the smaller trucks. Of course, all the neighbors read what each box contained and commented to each other.

The final news that spread fast throughout the village was that two professors from California were coming to establish a school in Cubuy. They saw the folding tables, the boxes of books, chalk, four chalkboards, and erasers. I had to stop various people to correct these news reports, affirming that I was a Puerto Rican and the other woman was an American. This did not change the news; it remained the news of that morning that two American professors had moved from California.

Returning to the Saturday morning sessions, John Luis brought more and more of his young male and female relatives to come on Saturday mornings. We moved from locating them into the universe, the world, the United States, and Puerto Rico, to speaking about the future and what they wanted to be. At first, there was very little anyone wanted to be, but after a while they stated their dreams of becoming a baker, making fancy cakes and sweet breads, or being an airline pilot or a surgeon. We were delighted, and talked about what we could do with this potential. One day, John Luis brought me a note from his aunt, who wished to meet me and Mina. We were invited to come to their house to meet her and her husband to talk about the Saturday sessions and what they were all about. When we went to visit, we were served guava paste on white Puerto Rican cheese and glasses of Coca Cola; this was customarily served to visitors in these mountain communities of Cubuy and Lomas. They asked questions, especially the uncle, and asked to know if we had been professors in California, but now were retired. Mina spoke in Spanish with an accent, but this was greatly appreciated. I explained that we could try to secure assistance for each of the youths to achieve the goals expressed in sessions with us. I asked permission from them to continue the meetings. They both agreed that the sessions should be continued; in fact, they offered an empty storefront under the living room where we were sitting, in case the group was too big for our porch. We thanked them for the refreshments and for the offer of space, and we left.

PRODUCIR, a Community Economic Development Project

Several weeks later, we received a message written on the letterhead of the Cubuy and Lomas Civic-Social Association to attend the next meeting of the association. They were asking us to talk about who we were, the school we were going to open in Cubuy, and what we were doing with the youth group on Saturday mornings. We felt a little apprehensive, but we attended the meeting on a Thursday evening at 7:00 P.M. The meeting was held in a small room next to the police station. There were about eighteen men dressed up in white *guayaberas* (a *guayabera* is a light cotton shirt with two panels of white embroidery on each side of the front buttons, ironed to perfection). The *guayaberas* were worn by men on formal occasions. There was only one woman in attendance, and she did not speak a word during the meeting. This was the situation with women at meetings, if they came at all. The meeting was presided by Tebo Meléndez, who had been the community organizer of a government program that taught rural communities to address community problems. He controlled the meeting by talking a lot. He described the projects that the association had successfully completed. I concluded his recounting of successful projects was for our benefit. He described how they had collected donations from the community to send a sick resident to a hospital in Texas for a treatment not available in Puerto Rico. He told of how they worked together to convert the water tank into an office for the association, which was the place where we were meeting. He mentioned other lesser projects and finally recounted how the community had insisted on having a police station in Cubuy to serve the two communities of Cubuy and Lomas. After the police authorities answered this request, saying this could not be done because there was no place to situate the station, they measured and drew the construction design of the police station in Canóvanas. A call was issued for all families in the two villages to donate cement blocks, cement, sand, paint, and tools, and to help construct the station over two weekends. The people built the police station using the model drawn. While the men worked in the construction, the women cooked a big dinner and fed the workers. After the station was built, they invited the police commander of the region from Carolina and handed him a key to the police station, with a petition for the services they expected. The president of the association told us that the police in the regional commanding area assigned three police officers to serve the area. Later on, they secured a policeman to organize a police athletic league chapter that was very successful with the teenagers in the villages.

We told them that we had come to retire. I said they were correct in thinking that we brought the furnishings, books, and papers of a school we had in California, but we were not going to open a school in Cubuy. When they asked about the sessions with the youths, I explained that we were community organizers and had a school to help youth learn how to resolve community problems. The president then said that they had been discussing us. They wished that we would work with the association to try to find a solution to a problem the youth of the community had. The youth had no source of employment after they graduated from school. At that moment, I felt that a community of my people was placing itself in our hands. In my profession, that type of situation was ideal. A community had asked community workers to help them resolve a problem they had identified.

Without talking to Mina, I knew she was thinking what I was thinking. In order to gain time to think, I said, "You have to select a committee of citizens that will work with us on this. We will not do this kind of work without the community working with us." My plan to postpone an answer to gain time did not work. The president of the association pointed to and called out seven of the members present and named them as a committee to work with the doctors in a project to solve the problems of the community. (The president, Tebo Meléndez, later became the mayor of Canóvanas.)

We left the meeting taking the names of the committee members and agreeing for a date, time, and place to meet with the committee. We met the following Thursday night at the office of the association. I realized that our plans for semiretirement had gone out the window. We met every Thursday for a year until a corporation was formed with a board and a plan of work designed by the group to address the problem of youth unemployment, as well as other problems identified during those sessions. I must confess that I felt greatly exhilarated and full of energy from our meetings. The men of this group quickly learned concepts we never thought they could understand. To us, the situation was ideal because we were doing community development with the methods and knowledge we had taught our students. We would discuss the work we were doing, correcting ourselves as we went along. Soon, the work became community economic development as the committee arrived at the conclusion that the village had no business that provided residents with the needed services that are basic to families.

Decisions were made to put into action a plan that was designed and approved by the committee to start the changes that were needed. In a year, the committee became a board of directors, learned how to hold meetings with an agenda, and called elections for officers of the board. We chose a name to symbolize the essence of the work we felt had to be done. Someone brought a quote from one of the great leaders of Puerto Rican history, Ramón Emeterio Betances: "Trabajar es producir y producir es servir a la humanidad" (to work is to produce and to produce is to serve humanity). The word *producir* was voted to be the name of the corporation. When PRODUCIR became a reality in Puerto Rico, there had been other efforts at community economic development that had been more or less successful. There had been the effort to develop a *parcha* juice cooperative in Guavate, a rural area near Guayama in the south. The most successful effort was Las Flores Metal Arte, a corporation that started as a metal furniture business and grew into a large corporation that manufactured wood furniture and kitchen cabinets. This last project was successful once it concentrated on its own development as a profit-generating enterprise and placed the original community development interests and activities in second place. The government and university professors had not developed a full understanding of the theoretical content needed to function successfully in the development of projects of this kind.

When PRODUCIR emerged, the political, governmental, and social leadership of the country was not fully aware or committed to learning about this kind of approach as a possible solution to the deteriorating conditions of poor people in urban and rural areas. The work that we did in Cubuy and Lomas in the thirteen years we were there becomes more meaningful as I think about it at a distance and try to answer questions about this endeavor. What did I want to do and why? How much of what was actually accomplished had anything to do with what I wanted to do? Was there a difference between what I wanted to accomplish and what the community wanted? How did the political and economic power struggles of Puerto Rico affect what we were able to accomplish? How much did our own need to bring closure to my feelings about Puerto Rico have to do with getting involved in the project to begin with and staying with it for such a long time? What I wanted to do in PRODUCIR was to bring together my philosophy, experience, and commitment in order to contribute to the country where I thought I belonged. I wanted to contribute solutions to the economic problems of Puerto Rico. This was a big mouthful and a grandiose undertaking. However, I have always thought this could be accomplished if each and every one of us who believes in it continues to work at it. The people in Cubuy and Lomas who worked closely with us as the staff and board had spoken to us about the general idea of social and economic justice—specifically about developing the local economy to be owned by individuals and the village community to create local wealth. They spoke about it and some worked to create it. Some of them understood it better than others. For some of them, individually and in groups, it became a reality in the creation of a bakery, a post office, a credit cooperative, several hydroponic systems for growing lettuce and selling it downtown—all producing income for sustaining their families. Finally, they also saw it in the construction of a shopping center that housed some of their businesses, a Head Start program to serve their children, and a program for high school students to enroll in colleges and universities.

What was not possible to accomplish and where did the responsibility lie? On me? On the people of the village? On the government of Puerto Rico or on the private funders? All levels of the government of Puerto Rico contributed to the failure of what we could not accomplish. The central government and its economic development agencies did not fund our training projects for entrepreneurs and did not approve our requests to invest in the creation of a bakery, the sewing factory, the health center, the hydroponic farms. The local, municipal government refused to build a road to link the shopping center, the housing project, and the health center to the main road. The local councilmen interfered with the mayor's support of the project, in general, because of their fear that maybe I would become a political leader to compete with them. We could not build the housing project or the health center, making it necessary to return thousands of dollars to federal agencies. Before I left, we returned $245,000 to Health and Human Services and did not accept a $150,000 grant from a bank in New York City. The Department of Housing and Urban Development had set aside $800,000 for the building of houses, and the Rural Development Agency (formerly Farmers Home Agency) had apportioned $300,000 for constructing the health clinic. All these monies could not be used.

The people of the village behaved in an ambivalent fashion, at times backing efforts to defend the project and at times attacking it. The churches in the villages (of which there were thirty-one fundamentalist Protestant churches of all denominations and one Catholic church) remained distant and at times negative to the project. The universities, the social agencies, the foundations, some banks, the corporations, and large industries were supportive of PRODUCIR, with funding and with general backing. The deeper problems of the island interfered with the development of the project. The political forces have not concerned themselves with the movement to create jobs, develop an island-based economy, and small businesses in local communities.

I had to come to Puerto Rico to try to do some community economic development work, as I had done in the United States. It was an inconclusive part of my life that had to be addressed. As I came to the decision to leave Puerto Rico again, first to leave the village and PRODUCIR, and later to move to New York again, I came to understand that community economic development, which is a difficult process to begin with, is impossible in the U.S.'s perfect colony. At that point, I understood fully the meaning of the book and study by Richard Weiskoff, *Factories and Food Stamps: The Puerto Rican Model of Development*, that analyzes the relationship of the Puerto Rican economy to the well-being of corporations of the United States as a reciprocal relationship in which local people are kept dependent upon welfare payments and food stamps that are given to be used to purchase goods shipped from the mainland.

Our work in Cubuy and Canóvanas allowed us to place into operation the values, commitments, and knowledge that had been secured through years of experience and teaching. In our chapter "Community Development and Restoration: A Perspective and Case Study," we presented these ideas in a text for social work students in community organizing. In this article, we proposed an analysis for assisting community practitioners in understanding processes of destruction imposed upon communities of the poor and oppressed. The case study continues to provide both a conceptual framework and strategy approaches for working with people as they plan and act to restore their communities to functional and productive arenas. We have always been mindful of the need for organizing activities and certainly value the models of

Alinsky and others. However, until recently, the field of community development, as distinct from community organizing, has had a paucity of models that address the tools for rebuilding. In our view, a great deal of the evolving literature and the work of funding sources has focused too narrowly on the development of technical skills rather than promoting and engaging people in the processes of empowerment and community building.

The field of community development has progressed greatly since we started, and many new workers have entered the arena. In our writings, we have a political analysis and a solid base of planning action tools. It is our strong belief that commitment, energy, and analysis must be accompanied by a solid base of knowledge about communities and community functioning. We owe it to the people with whom we work to use these tools, also knowing full well the power and determination of those who are powerful and seek to sustain conditions of inequality.

The PRODUCIR model of community economic development produced several significant, professional outcomes. The conceptual and practical development of a model for community development was recognized in a short documentary produced by CNN. A short teaching documentary, *Fields of Dreams*, was produced as a teaching document for work in developing nations. We were invited to participate in the publication of a text that is used by schools of social work. Our chapter, "Community Development and Restoration: A Perspective and Case Study," is used as a basic reference for students in the community practice sequences. We were invited to present the community economic development model to policy specialists from the University of Havana, Cuba, and to a training seminar for community workers in Bogotá, Columbia.

Another very important result from PRODUCIR has been the development of two corporations that continue the community work in Cubuy and Lomas and the urban area of San Juan. PRO-Vivienda, Inc., is a corporation that owns four buildings that house low- and moderate-income families. These buildings were purchased with mortgage guarantees from HUD to insure that the 912 families who are residents would be able to keep their homes instead of being displaced for high rental conversions or luxury condominiums. The new board, created by PRODUCIR to own and manage the buildings, has a commitment to keeping these buildings as homes for current residents and/or other residents of comparable income levels. The board of PRODUCIR also created PRODECO, a community trust to support community development activities. The trust offers skill training and assists in the development of small businesses of nontraditional owners. The trust is managed by an independent board, of which I continue as a member.

Third Emigration: The Return to New York City

I knew that I did not belong in Puerto Rico. I discussed it with Mina, raising the question, "Where do I belong? Where do we go now?" The answer would become clear. I belong in New York with Nuyoricans. They are the family that I built for myself once upon a time. I had left New York a long time ago, but now I must return. For a short time, Mina and I considered living in downtown San Juan. We considered living in Old San Juan, but settled for a condominium on the beach in Isla Verde, close to San Juan. We found a condominium apartment that had a view of the large lagoon and the three peaks of El Yunque on one side and the large blue ocean on the other side. We felt that life in Isla Verde would offer more opportunity for enjoying cultural activities and contacts with friends. This was not enough for us. We needed a more varied social and cultural life. During the thirteen years in the hills, we had felt deprived of these experiences. We could walk from the building to the beach. The beach was beautiful and can have a calming effect that wipes away all the problems of the island.

We started the work of preparing a transition committee for my leaving PRODUCIR. I used the consultation of the transition committee, a lawyer, and an accountant to prepare the necessary steps for our leaving and for a new group, including the resident board, to control the operation of the programs.

One year following this decision, we left the island and returned to New York. This trip was our homecoming.

Epilogue

Reflections and Ruminations

Writing these memoirs has been an integrating activity. As I come to the end of this adventure that I started two years ago, I contemplate the road traveled and find myself at peace, because of various reasons. First, the reflection and writing have allowed me to integrate many pieces of myself that had been disconnected. I have also been able to resolve many old issues. I understand and accept how I have felt about my mother and how she has felt about me. I have an understanding of why we were distant toward each other in a way that we could never correct prior to her death. Many issues of love and anger with my mother were addressed through these memoirs. I only wish that I could have had the opportunity to let her know that I saw her as an adventurous and brave woman who was ahead of her time. I wish that I could have told her that I admired her strengths and determination.

Another very important piece of the integrating process has been my ability to accept who I am, with my shortcomings and faults. I know that my faults and shortcomings have been carefully tied to my strengths. I know, for example, that I can be a Dionysian extremist who can immerse herself in the enjoyment of the senses. The Dionysian self has been kept under control by the builder of institutions and the careful planner, who is also me. I must confess that there has always been another part of me that I have not fully developed. This is the poet in me, who has been waiting for freedom and an opportunity for expression. During the writing of my memoirs, I searched my old files and I found my old poems. I have never shared them with anyone.

The Tropics
(1942, age 20, Puerto Rico)

Sparks of lightning tear the shadows
Beams of moonlight erase the gloomy darkness
Caresses of soft warm breezes touch and surround
Languor of overflowing star nights
All these are the tropics.

Wild waves of tempestuous seas
Incessant displays of rainy evenings
Voluptuous indifference of laziness
All these are the tropics.

Possessing the Virgin Image
(1942, age 20, Puerto Rico)

Dark and virgin image, yield to me
That the hands may strangle desire
In soft, tremulous caress

In the agonizing violence of a tender kiss
In opening prayer, yield to me so that
In the act of deflowering,
The sacrificed soul
My anxious hands may gather
When you yield to me.

Dark and virgin image, yield to me
That I might destroy want
with enveloping embrace.

Vision
(September 1947, age 25, NYC)

I had a vision
And it was an immense floating blue green
And it was a soft, soft floating cloud
And it was a lovely floating quietness
And it was a floating fountain of love
And it was all beauty and all kindness

And all that I saw in it
Made my heart spill over with warm tenderness
made in my eyes a light of joy glow
And I wanted to let you see
And I wanted to let you feel
And I wanted to share with you
but then, I stopped to look again
And it was just a vision.

The Moon
(August 1947, age 25, NYC)

The moon is you
The moon is my eternal lover
It wanders in my nights
It hangs over into my days

The moon is my beloved
The moon with its green eyes
It drives me into summits of ecstasy
It's still there in my lowest sadness

These clumsy and immature efforts remained in my old boxes of papers for many years. I never disposed of them because I have had a childlike attachment to them, always thinking that maybe at a future time I could return to polish them.

Many people have called me a visionary. I never liked this characterization because I considered my ideas and projects practical answers to the resolution of problems. Now, I accept that I am a visionary, if being a visionary means that I have tried to transform reality.

I said in the beginning of these reflections and ruminations that I find myself at peace. Although I have not discussed directly my sexuality, I am also at peace with this part of me. I have decided not to discuss it in this book because I have always drawn a line between my private and public life. However, I wish to eliminate the possibility of being misinterpreted and being described as secretive about this matter. I claim it at various points throughout the book.

I am at peace with who I am . . . with my achievements and with the manner in which I have handled and corrected my mistakes. I have come to realize that, in a great measure, one becomes who one wishes to make oneself. I have created my own definition of myself to avoid having others define me. However, there are some given factors and realities that must be taken into consideration, but one must not allow them to become limiting obstacles. These obstacles are part of the constant and changing reality, but I have chosen to view them as surmountable, providing me with opportunities for enhancing and transforming my life. The most important achievement in the process of integration has been finding the answer that I have carried within me for many years and over many spans of geography: "Where is my home?" I now know that home is New York City. I have returned and resumed my work in my community with old friends and new friends. I am a Nuyorican!

Bibliography

Blourock, Barbara, James Bowman, and Antonia Pantoja, eds. *Badges and Indicia of Slavery: Cultural Pluralism Redefined*. Lincoln: Cultural Pluralism Committee, Study Commission on Undergraduate Education and the Education of Teachers, 1975.

——, Pablo Figueroa, and Antonia Pantoja, eds. *Events in the History of Puerto Rico*. New York: Research for Urban Education, Inc., 1967.

Pantoja, Antonia. "A Guide for Action in Intergroup Relations." *Social Group Work: Selected Papers from the National Conference on Social Welfare,* 1961.

——, and Wilhelmina Perry. "A Third World Perspective: A New Paradigm for Social Science Research." *Research: A Third World Perspective, Western Interstate Commission for Higher Education.* 1967. 1–17.

——. "Community Development and Restoration: A Perspective and Case Study." *Community Organizing in a Diverse Society.* Eds. John L. Erlich and Félix G. Rivera. Boston: Allyn and Bacon, 1998. 220–242.

——. "Cultural Pluralism, A Goal to be Realized." *Voices From the Battlefront: Achieving Cultural Equity.* Eds. Marta Moreno Vega and Cheryll Greene. New Jersey: Africa World Press Inc., 1993. 135–148.

——. "Social Work in a Culturally Pluralistic Society: An Alternative Paradigm." *Cross-Cultural Perspectives in Social Work Practice.* Houston: University of Houston, 1976. 79–95.

——. "The University: An Institution for Community Development." *Coming Home: Community-based Education and the Development of Communities*. Washington, D.C.: Clearing House for Community-based, Free-standing Educational Institutions, 1979. 28–33.

———. "Toward the Development of Theory: Cultural Pluralism Redefined." *Journal of Sociology and Social Welfare* IV (1976): 125–146.

Perry, Wilhelmina. "Memories of a Life of Work: An Interview with Antonia Pantoja." *Harvard Educational Review. Symposium: Colonialism and Working-Class Resistance: Puerto Rican Education in the United States* 68 (1998): 244–258.

Puerto Rican Forum. *Poverty Conditions of the Puerto Rican Community of New York City*. New York: Puerto Rican Forum, Inc., 1965.

Additional titles in our

Hispanic Civil Rights Series

Message to Aztlán
Rodolfo "Corky" Gonzales
ISBN 1-55885-331-6

A Gringo Manual on How to Handle Mexicans
José Angel Gutiérrez
ISBN 1-55885-326-X

Eyewitness: A Filmmaker's Memoir of the Chicano Movement
Jesús Treviño
ISBN 1-55885-349-9

Pioneros puertorriqueños en Nueva York, 1917–1947
Joaquín Colón
ISBN 1-55885-335-9

The American GI Forum: In Pursuit of the Dream, 1948–1983
Henry Ramos
Clothbound, ISBN 1-55885-261-1
Trade Paperback, ISBN 1-55885-262-X

Chicano! The History of the Mexican American Civil Rights Movement
F. Arturo Rosales
ISBN 1-55885-201-8

Testimonio: A Documentary History of the Mexican-American Struggle for Civil Rights
F. Arturo Rosales
ISBN 1-55885-299-9

They Called Me "King Tiger": My Struggle for the Land and Our Rights
Reies López Tijerina
ISBN 1-55885-302-2

Julian Nava: My Mexican-American Journey
Julian Nava
Clothbound, ISBN 1-55885-364-2
Trade Paperback, ISBN 1-55885-351-0